Please note the information contained within this document is for educational and entertainment purposes only. All effort has been executed to present accurate, up to date, reliable, complete information. No warranties of any kind are declared or implied. Readers acknowledge that the author is not engaged in the rendering of legal, financial, medical, or professional advice. The content within this book has been derived from various sources. Please consult a licensed professional before attempting any techniques outlined in this book. By reading this document, the reader agrees that under no circumstances is the author responsible for any losses, direct or indirect, that are incurred as a result of the use of the information contained within this document, including, but not limited to, errors, omissions, or inaccuracies.

CONTENTS

Introduction

The human body is a combination of several organs, and each organ plays an important role. People often ignore the role of gallbladder because they do not know about its importance. Remember, the gallbladder is essential for your biliary system. It is responsible for storage, transportation and production of bile. The liver works hard to make the bile that is essential for digestion. Your gallbladder holds this bile until your body needs it.

The liver produces a yellowish-brown fluid known as bile. Gallbladder hangs out below the right lobe of the liver.However, this pear-shaped organ is not vital for your survival because there are other ways to supply bile to the small intestine. Sometimes, it becomes crucial to surgically remove this small organ because of pain or other problems. Some associated issues with this little organ are gallstones, gallbladder disease and gallbladder attack.

Remember, cholangitis, pancreatitis, cholecystitis, biliary colic and gallstones can be the reason for gallbladder pain. The gallbladder acts as storage for bile if it is not needed for digestion. The absorbent lining of gallbladder concentrates the bike. Once the food comes to your small intestine, cholecystokinin (a hormone) is released and signals the gallbladder to secrete bile in the small intestine through a bile duct.

The bile can break up digestive fats and drain waste products from your liver to the duodenum. Gallstones can be formed because of extra bile salt, bilirubin and cholesterol. These are small and hard deposits in your gallbladder. Numerous people may not notice the symptoms of small gallstones. Large gallstones can increase discomfort, and surgery becomes necessary to remove them.

If you want to avoid all these conditions, manage a healthy diet. You have to eat a balanced diet with vegetables, fruits, fiber and lean meats. For a healthy gallbladder, you have to follow a low-fat and low-cholesterol diet. Remember, food items good for your cardiovascular health are suitable for gallbladder. After removing the gallbladder, you may experience several painful symptoms.

Some people may not notice anything after ditching this small organ. By removing the gallbladder, you will remove this small reservoir. The bile will be released directly in the small intestine. After your surgery, the doctor may recommend you to eat a low-fat diet. It will help your body to adjust your life without a gallbladder.

You have to manage digestive problems after your surgery. Some medicines are available for your assistance. Here are some notable lifestyle changes.

● Start following a low-fat diet
● Prevent fatty foods, including fried foods
● Eat frequent, small meals
● Avoid a large meal after fasting for a day

In this book, you will find essential lifestyle changes after removing the gallbladder. Moreover, it has a diet plan and 100 delicious recipes to stay healthy and happy. The meal plan and recipes are tried and tested for anyone living without a gallbladder. Fortunately, these recipes are useful for everyone who wants to avoid gallbladder diseases.

Best Diet for Healthy Gallbladder:

Avoid Gallbladder Diseases

Undoubtedly, the gallbladder is not essential to keep your body functioning and healthy. Most people may not realize the development of gallstones. Remember, gallstones may trigger different symptoms, including vomiting, nausea, bloating and abdominal pain. The symptoms may be recurrent and frequent. The ultimate treatment is surgery to remove this organ.

Several risk factors add to the development of gallstones, such as gender and family history. Women are more prone to develop gallstone as compared to men. Bodyweight is an essential factor because obesity can increase the chances of gallstone development. Moreover, low fiber and high fat in the diet can be the main culprit. You can avoid problems in the gallbladder by changing your diet.

If you are obese, make sure to reduce your weight gradually. Avoid quick weight loss because it can trigger gallstone formation. Crash diets stimulate the liver to release extra cholesterol into bile and disrupt your hormonal balance. The additional cholesterol may turn into crystals and form gallstones.

If you want to keep your gallbladder healthy, you have to eat a well-balanced diet with lean meats, vegetables, fiber and fruits. Your body needs fresh vegetables and fiber-rich fruits. The diet must decrease the stress from your gallbladder. Some healthy items are legumes, spices, nuts, whole grains, low-fat dairy items, vegetables and fresh fruits.

Olive Oil to Keep Your Gallbladder Healthy

Olive oil is healthy for your heart and gallbladder. It is a reliable source of unsaturated fats to prompt your small organs to empty. By adding olive oil in your diet, you can decrease the chances of gallbladder diseases. Make sure to use olive oil instead of butter. Choose healthy fats to keep your gallbladder healthy, such as avocadoes, nuts and salmon.

Vegetables and Fruits

You will need gallbladder friendly fruits and vegetables, such as cranberries, avocadoes, grapes, beets and berries. Oranges, bell peppers and broccoli, have vitamin C and fiber. Lack of this vitamin can increase the chances of gallstone. Moreover, pectin-rich fruits are suitable for your gallbladder, such as citrus, strawberries and apples. Radishes are appropriate options to increase the flow of bile. If you are suffering from gallbladder problems, avoid consuming radishes.

Poultry, Fish and Meat

The rounds or loins have less fat; therefore, these cuts are safe for your health. Any skinless chicken, lamb or fish are good choices for you. Protein is vital for the growth and repair of body tissues.

Dairy products and red meat offer sufficient protein to your body. Remember, they are high in fat; therefore, you have to be careful. High-fat diet can increase stress on your gallbladder. Avoid processed food because these have high salt. Fresh foods are healthy options because of limited sugar.

Whole Grains

You can consume soy products, soy, seeds, nuts, legumes and soy milk. Moreover, healthy whole grains include brown rice, bran cereal and oats. Prefer cereals and bread containing several grains and high fiber. Focus on the fat content of dairy food items.

Live an Active Life

Physical activity is necessary to burn fat and shed extra pounds. It will help you to boost mood, protect gallbladder and boost mood. By exercising regularly, you can decrease the chances of gallbladder disease. Feel free to start jogging, running or walking as per your convenience.

Alcohol and Caffeinated Coffee

For a healthy gallbladder, you have to decrease the amount of caffeine or alcohol. It will reduce the danger of gallstones. Make sure to restrict caffeine from other sources, including soda and tea. Researchers have mixed reviews about caffeinated drinks. For this reason, avoid excessive consumption of caffeine.

Drink Sufficient Water

No doubt, hydration is essential to manage sufficient water in your bile. Your body needs water to keep organs happy. Some people drink eight glasses of water daily as a healthy goal. Remember, this amount may vary in each person. If you are drinking less water than the actual requirements of your body, your gallbladder will be at risk.

Water can keep organs empty and avoid buildup from bile. It offers protection against gallstone and several other problems. By drinking more water, you can shed extra pounds. If you are drinking more water, you will eat less sugar and few calories.

Consume Nuts

Some studies prove that tree nuts and peanuts can help you to avoid gallstones. It is essential to restrict the consumption of nuts. Eating too many nuts may increase fat content in your body. Nuts have healthy fat and fiber along with plant sterols. This compound can block the absorption of cholesterol in your body. Make sure to eat almost one ounce of nuts 5 times per week to avoid gallstones. You can consume nuts as snacks or sprinkle them on salad, cereals and other dishes. When consuming nuts, it is essential to keep an eye on your calories.

Eat Plant-based Foods

A healthy diet offers several nutrients to your body. You will get antioxidants, minerals, and vitamins from plant-based foods. It allows you to avoid gallbladder diseases. Remember, antioxidants are useful for your body to prevent toxic molecules, such as free radicals.

Your body can develop free radicals because of environmental stresses and natural processes, such as processed foods. The build-up of free radicals may increase the chances of oxidative stress. It can increase the chances of cell damage that will be the reason for cancer and several other diseases.

Source of Minerals and Calcium

To support the health of your gallbladder, you will need calcium and minerals. Plenty of calcium in your diet is excellent for the health of your gallbladder. Calcium is available in broccoli, kale, and other leafy, dark greens. Moreover, it is available in milk, cheese, and yogurt. Some fortified alternatives to dairy are flax milk or almond. For your gallbladder, orange juice and sardines are some excellent choices. If you are suffering from gallbladder disease, you must consume dairy products with zero fat.

Moreover, your body needs folate, magnesium and vitamin C to prevent gallbladder issues. Fresh vegetables and fruits offer these nutrients. You can find vitamin C in citrus foods, oranges, green and red peppers, broccoli, kiwifruit, tomatoes, and strawberries. Remember, vitamin C is soluble in water; therefore, cooking veggies in vitamin C can remove it from your food. Vegetables, raw and fresh fruits are great sources of vitamin C.

If you want magnesium, you can consume cashews, almonds, peanut butter, peanuts, beans, spinach, edamame, potato, soy milk, rice, avocado, banana and yogurt. Furthermore, your body needs folate, and excellent sources of folate are beef liver, black-eyed peas, spinach, fortified cereals, and asparagus. No doubt, you can get these minerals from supplements, but try to get them from fresh dietary sources.

Foods to Avoid to Keep Your Gallbladder Healthy

Modern western diet can trigger different gallbladder symptoms. This diet is high in saturated fats and refined carbohydrates. If you are noticing symptoms of gallstones, you have to focus on the health of your gallbladder. Remember, gallstones can impact the outflow of bile reserved in your gallbladder. You can make the situation worse by eating fatty food items.

After developing gallstones, you can't get rid of them with a healthy diet. Surgical treatments are necessary to remove them. Remember, a balanced and healthy diet will help you to avoid gallstones. Balanced nutrients, limited saturated fats and food with heavy cholesterol can help you to ease symptoms. Make sure to limit or avoid high-fat foods in your regular diet, such as:

●Cookies, pie, doughnuts (highly processed foods)
●Fried foods
●Dairy products with whole-milk (butter, ice cream, cheese)
●Red meat with high fat

If you are overweight, try to reduce weight slowly, such as 1 – 2 pounds per week. Make sure to consult your doctor before following a diet. Avoid fatty and fried foods to avoid gallstones.

Refined Carbohydrates and Sugar

Refined carbohydrates, sugar and sweetener, are unhealthy for you. To protect your gallbladder, you have to avoid refined sugars and high-fructose corn syrup. Sugar and refined carbohydrates are frequently found in snack foods, soda and cookies.

Canned or frozen vegetables and fruits have additives; therefore, your gallbladder finds it challenging to work on them. You should not consume foods with white flour, such as desserts, pasta, white bread, etc. Moreover, processed snacks are not healthy for your gallbladder, such as pies, cookies and potato chips.

Remember, every packed snack is terrible for your entire body. You have to decrease the consumption of high-fat foods, including fatty meat cuts, fried food, dairy products, etc. It is essential to avoid processed food items. For the protection of your gallbladder, you can follow a low-fat diet. Avoid following an extremely low-calorie diet. By eating 1,000 or less calories per day, you can trigger the formation of gallstone.

Cleanse Your Body

Gallbladder cleansing is a necessary remedy to treat gallstones. Make sure to skip food and drink fresh juices, herbal water and olive oil. In this way, you can break up maximum gallstones to pee them out. Before cleansing your body, it will be great to consult your doctor. Sometimes, cleansing can trigger diarrhea, nausea and stomach pain.

How to live after removing gallbladder from your body?

If you are experiencing symptoms of gallstones, removal of the gallbladder can solve this problem. No doubt, the gallbladder is not essential for your body, but the body requires time to adjust without a gallbladder. Your body may not accept fatty foods. Once your gallbladder is removed, you will experience watery stools. In numerous cases, diarrhea lasts for 15 to 30 days.

You should not worry about diarrhea because bile is directly releasing in your intestine after removing the gallbladder. Now the bile will be drained continuously in your intestine in a less concentrated form. The amount of fat in your diet can impact your digestion. A large amount of fat may cause diarrhea, bloating and gas. Fortunately, you can protect yourself from different problems with the help of these precautions.

Avoid High-Fat Diets

You should avoid consuming grease, fried and high-fat food items. Moreover, stay away from gravies and fatty sauces for almost one week after surgery. Your diet should not have over 3 grams of fat. After surgery, stick to liquids, gelatin and broths. You can slowly add solid foods again to your diet. Stick to small and frequent meals instead of gas-causing and pungent odor foods. By avoiding fried food, you can say goodbye to discomfort. Here are some essential items to avoid:

●Pizza
●Potato chips and French fries
●High-fat meats, including ground beef, sausage and bologna
●High-fat dairy, including whole milk, ice cream and cheese
●Butter and lard
●Creamy sauces and soups
●Chocolate
●Meat gravies
●Oils, including palm and coconut oil
●Turkey or chicken skin
●Spicy foods

Try to consume less than 60 grams of healthy fat. Carefully read labels of food items before consuming them.

Slowly Increase Fiber In Your Diet

Fiber is essential to normalize your bowel movements. You can increase soluble fiber in your diet, including barley and oats. Slowly increase fiber to your diet, such as numerous weeks. Remember, the excessive fiber in your diet can increase cramping and gas issues. It is important to go easy with gas-producing foods, such as:

●Nuts
●Legumes
●Whole-grain bread
●Seeds
●Broccoli
●Brussels sprouts
●Cabbage
●Cereal
●Cauliflower

Slowly add these items in your diet in small quantities. Avoid reintroducing them quickly to decrease the chances of bloating, cramping and diarrhea.

Maintain a Food Journal

After surgery, you can maintain a food journal to track what you are eating and impact of your diet on your body. It will help you to find out your food allergies and other issues. Some people may take only one month to return to their normal diet. You should consult your doctor after experiencing any of these symptoms:

●Jaundice

●Severe vomiting or nausea

●Consistent or severe pain in abdomen

●Missing bowel movements for almost three or more days after surgery

●Persistent diarrhea after surgery

●Incapability to pass gas after surgery

After surgery, you may feel comfortable by passing gas. Over time, your tolerance for fats and high-fiber food will increase. It is the right time to add healthy food items back to your diet.

Be Careful about Dairy

Dairy and milk products provide your body with protein, vitamin D and calcium. Remember, this food group may increase troubles after gallbladder surgery.

If you want to avoid an upset digestive system, select fat-free or low-fat dairy products. Your body needs low-fat cheese and skim milk. Avoid drinking whole-milk dairy items because its content can increase the chances of diarrhea. Moreover, low-fat yogurt is good for digestion because of living, active bacterial cultures.

Avoid Dehydration

If you are experiencing diarrhea after surgery, you should focus on hydration. Remember, diarrhea may drain fluids, minerals and vitamins from your body. For this reason, drink sufficient water and fresh juices to increase minerals and vitamins in your body. Sports drinks may help you in diarrhea because of their chloride, potassium and sodium content. Avoid caffeine and alcohol, including soft drinks, tea and coffee.

Natural Remedies to Relieve Gallbladder Pain

Unhealthy eating habits and wrong lifestyle can be the reason for gallbladder pain. You can decrease the burden on your liver and pancreas by eating healthy food and limiting fat intake. Regular exercise can reduce cholesterol levels and the formation of gallstones. As mentioned earlier, fried foods and condiments with fats are not allowed. Fats in these foods are difficult to break down and increase pain.

Make sure to include nutrient-rich meals in your diet, including fruits and vegetables. These can improve the function of your gallbladder and avoid complications. Here are some natural remedies to deal with gallbladder issues. Remember, these are temporary solutions; therefore, you should consult a doctor for your proper treatment.

Heated Compress

Apply heat to relieve and soothe pain because heated compresses can relieve unnecessary pressure and calm spasms. To relieve pain, soak a towel in warm water and squeeze extra liquid. Apply this wet towel to an affected area for almost 10 – 15 minutes.

You can get the same effects with the use of a hot water bottle or heating pad. Replicate this procedure until you start feeling good. Avoid putting this towel directly on your skin because it can be harmful. Moreover, hot water bottles, heating pads and heated compresses are available easily.

Peppermint Tea

Peppermint has menthol to relieve pain. Remember, menthol is a soothing element to promote pain relief.You can use it to improve digestion, relieve nausea and ease pain in the stomach. For the treatment of gallbladder pain, drink this tea regularly. Regular use of this tea will be useful to decrease the pain attacks of the gallbladder.

Apple Cider Vinegar

In raw apple cider vinegar, you will find anti-inflammatory benefits. It is useful to relieve the pain of your gallbladder. If you want to treat gallbladder pain, dissolve almost two tablespoons of vinegar in warm water. Drink this mixture to subside pain without any side effect. Avoid drinking vinegar straight because it is dangerous for your teeth.

Turmeric

For the treatment of different health conditions, turmeric has numerous health benefits. Turmeric has curcumin that is famous for its healing and anti-inflammatory benefits. It can stimulate the formation of bile and ease emptying of the gallbladder. Incorporate this herb in your diet to decrease gallbladder pain and inflammation. For pain relief, you can add turmeric in your tea. Fortunately, you can find curcumin oral supplement. Before using a dietary supplement, you should discuss its benefits and risks with your doctor.

Magnesium Supplement

Magnesium proves helpful to promote emptying gallbladder. It may ease the pain and spasms of the gallbladder. Deficiency of this mineral can increase the danger of gallstone formation. To alleviate its symptoms, mix one teaspoon of magnesium powder in milk and drink after every few hours. Oral supplements of magnesium are available in the market. Consult your doctor before using any supplement or an appropriate dose of magnesium.

Before using any natural remedy, you should remember that natural treatments can soothe the pain of gallbladder. With natural remedies, you cannot ignore traditional therapies. Home remedies are useful to decrease symptoms related to gallbladder infection and disease. These remedies will not treat any underlying problem.

Natural Remedies for Treatment of Gallstones

Gallstones are firm deposits in your gallbladders, such as pigment gallstones and cholesterol gallstones. Undoubtedly, surgery is necessary to remove gallstones, but you can try natural remedies to relieve their symptoms. For your assistance, here are some natural remedies to prevent these conditions. It is essential to talk with a doctor before treating gallstones with these remedies. With the help of a doctor, you can correctly diagnose the treatment of your problem.

Gallbladder Cleanse

In the first step, you have to find out the reasons for gallstones. The liver can secrete extra bile than its capability to dissolve. The body has excess pigment known as bilirubin, and it cannot be completely dissolved. If your gallbladder is not emptying completely, it will form gallstones.

Some people use olive oil, herbs and juice for two or even more days. They consume oil mixtures throughout the day. Remember, this mixture can be dangerous for diabetic people. Olive oil can impact your bile consumption, but it has no impacts on gallstones. Before selecting any cleanser, you have to consult your doctor.

Apple Juice

Apple juice is useful for the treatment of gallstones. People believe that apple juice can make gallstones soft and help them pass through your urine. There is no scientific evidence to support this claim. If you have stomach ulcers, hypoglycemia and diabetes, fruit juices can be harmful to you.

Apple Cider Vinegar

Apple cider vinegar is a famous health supplement available to cleanse your body. It may offer several positive impacts on your blood sugar. People believe that it is useful for gallstone treatments, but scientific evidence is not available.

Milk Thistle

It is useful to treat gallbladder and liver disorders. You can use this flowering herb to stimulate organs. This herb is available in different supplements. Make sure to ask your doctor if you need this herb. Use of this herb will help you to decrease blood sugar levels in individuals with type II diabetes. Some people can be allergic to milk thistle.

Artichoke

Artichoke is beneficial for the function of your gallbladder. It can stimulate bile because artichoke has several benefits for your liver. You can grill, pickle or steam artichoke as per your taste. If you can tolerate artichoke, it can be a healthy addition to your diet.

Gold Coin Grass

Lysimachia herba or gold coin grass is a traditional Chinese medicine for the treatment of gallstones. It proves helpful to decrease the formation of gallstone. People prefer to use this grass for gallstone cleansing. This grass is available in liquid and powder form. Important Note: You should not use any of these remedies without consulting your doctor. There is no scientific evidence to prove the benefits of these herbs and minerals. Scientists and researchers do not confirm their effects on gallstones.

30 Days Diet Plan to Keep Gallbladder Healthy

Day	Breakfast	AM SNACK	Lunch	PM SNACK	Dinner
Day 1	Herbal Eggs + 1 glass juice	1 Fruit + Herbal Tea	Low-fat Pizza + Salad	Chicken Salad	Chicken with walnut seeds
Day 2	Spinach Frittata + Toast	Hummus and Vegetables	Rice + Tortilla and Cheesy Casserole	Apple + Peanut Butter	Creamy Chicken Salsa + Vegetable Rice
Day 3	1 Cheesy Pancake+ 1 cup of tea	Fruity Shake	Dessert of Your Choice	Hummus + Vegetable	Broiled Fish with Brown Sugar + Salad
Day 4	Vegetable Noodles + Smoothie	Vegetable and Hummus	Sandwich + Fruit	10 Almonds + 1 Fruit	Cabbage Steak + Juice
Day 5	Cauliflower Salad + 1 Fruit	A Dessert Bar	Chicken Salad	Glazed Carrots and Juice	Broccoli with Cheese and Egg Noodles + Milk
Day 6	Avgolemono + brown bread	Almond + Smoothie	Frittata + Salad	Milkshake	Soup + Salad
Day 7	Fruity Yogurt + 1 Servings of Spaghetti Squash	Egg White + Almonds	Zucchini Pasta + Fruit Salad	Hummus + 1 Toast	Chicken kabobs and cauliflower rice
Day 8	2 Pancakes + Herbal Tea	Roasted Pistachio 7 to 8	Avocado Smoothie	Handful Almonds	Chicken Wings
Day 9	Chocolate Milk + 1 Fruit	10 Raisins	Chicken Salad	Tuna Patty	Zucchini
Day 10	Smoothie + Hamburger Patty	Dessert Bar	Cauliflower Rice	7 – 8 Almonds	Pasta + Salad
Day 11	Chocolate Bomb + 1 Glass of Juice	1 Brownie	Chicken Salad	1 Apple	Soup + 1 toast
Day 12	1 Glass of Smoothie + Cauliflower Rice	Toasted Almonds 10	Dessert Treat	Toasted Seeds 7 to 8	Salmon Patty
Day 13	Fruit Salad + Smoothie	Buttery Carrots	Salsa and juice	½ Avocado	Healthy Pasta
Day 14	Cinnamon Treat + Green Juice	Toasted Almonds	1 Serving of soup	Apple Juice	Chicken
Day 15	Summer Squash + Cucumber Juice	Toast + Spread	Salad + Blueberries	Olives + Egg Salad	Grilled Chicken + Bread Toast
Day 16	Pancakes + 1 glass smoothie	Toasted Almonds	Potato Salad	Smoothie	Chicken Nuggets
Day 17	1 cup oats + Orange juice + Chocolate milk	Mixed dried fruits	Gherkins Salad	Chicken Skewer	Tangy Fillets + Rice
Day 18	Baked Eggs + Cabbage Juice	Toasted sunflower	Healthy Pasta	10 Peanuts	Steak + Rice

		seeds		
Day 19	Aloe Vera Juice + Egg White	Roasted Vegetables	Chicken Salad	**Watercress Sandwich**	Noodles and soup
Day 20	Pancake + Fruit Salad	Handful Blueberries	Tacos + Fruit	Peanut bars	Fish fillet
Day 21	Avocado + Green Smoothie	Toasted Almonds	Egg and Tomato Salad	Salad + Sandwich	Chicken Balls + Vegetable Rice
Day 22	Low-fat Pancake + Green Smoothie	Fruity chicken salad	Tilapia with Cheese	½ apple and ½ Banana	Roasted Chicken and salad
Day 23	Baked Egg + 1 cup fruit salad	Handful Blueberries	Vegetable Salad	Fat Bomb	Vegan Steak
Day 24	Muffin + Green Smoothie	Low-carb cookies	Wonton Wrapper	Toasted almonds	Bacon and Cabbage
Day 25	1 cup oats + Chocolate Milk	1 Avocado	Fruit Salad and nuts	Beans salad	Salmon Patties + Salad
Day 26	Fruity Salad + Pancakes	Spread + Toast	Cauliflower Rice + Chicken Salad	Almond milk	Chicken soup
Day 27	Bread Slices + Eggs	Toasted almonds	Delicious chicken Salad	Gherkins Salad	Fish + Salad
Day 28	Pancakes and smoothie	Almond bars	Vegetable and fruit salad	Carrot+ Juice	Spinach Soup and noodles
Day 29	1 cup Juice + Salad	½ Avocado	Sandwich + Date + 10 Nuts	Juice	Chicken fillet + Fruit Salad
Day 30	Spinach Omelet + Plain Yogurt	Cashew Nuts	Pie + Apple	Fruity Smoothie	Roasted Meat

Gallbladder Breakfast Recipes

For a healthy gallbladder, you have to start your day with a healthy breakfast. Here are some delicious recipes to start your day.

Recipe 01: Delicious Herbal Eggs

Cooking Time: 10 minutes

Servings: 8

Ingredients

- 1 ½ tablespoons butter
- 8 eggs
- 2 tablespoons water or milk
- Salt
- ½ cup chopped parsley and tarragon
- Ground black pepper
- Scallions (green parts)

DIRECTIONS:

1.   Heat a nonstick pan on medium flame and pour butter into it. Let the butter melt. Meanwhile, whisk eggs in a bowl with pepper, salt and milk.

2.   Pour this mixture in the pan and let it cook for 3 to 4 minutes. Turn the eggs upside down and sprinkle with green scallions and herbs. Serve hot.

Nutritional Information Per Serving:

183.2 total calories, 13.6-gram fat, 5.38 grams sat fat, 432.64 mg cholesterol, 370.31 mg sodium, 13 mg protein, 1.5 g carbohydrates, 0.23 g fiber, 2.23 mg iron and 69.64 mg calcium

Recipe 02: Spinach Frittata

Cooking Time: 40 minutes
Servings: 8
Ingredients:
- 3 tablespoons Olive oil
- 2 teaspoons salt or as per taste
- 10 whole eggs
- ½ teaspoon ground pepper
- 5-ounce baby spinach
- 1-pint grape tomatoes (Slices)
- 8ounces feta, crushed
- 4 scallions (sliced)

DIRECTIONS:
1. Preheat your oven to 350° F. Add oil in a baking casserole and put it in preheated oven for almost 5 minutes.
2. Whisk pepper, salt and eggs together in a bowl.
3. Keep it in the oven for 5 minutes. Meanwhile, whisk eggs in a bowl after adding pepper and salt. Mix in tomato, scallions and spinach as well.
4. Add feta in eggs and keep the bowl aside. Take out casserole from the oven. Pour in whisked eggs into casserole and bake for 25 to 30 minutes to get puffed eggs.

Nutritional Information:
461 total calories, 65 g fat, 579 mg cholesterol, 1,868 mg sodium, 26 g protein, 8 g carbohydrate, 5 g sugar, and 2 g fiber

Recipe 03: Baked Herbal Egg

Cooking Time: 20 minutes

Servings: 4

Ingredients:

•1 tablespoon soft butter

•8 tablespoons cream (low fat)

•8 whole eggs

•Salt to taste

•Ground black pepper

•1 tablespoon chopped parsley and dill

•Toast to serve

DIRECTIONS:

1.   Preheat an oven to 425° F. Take eight ramekins and coat each ramekin with cream.

2.   Break two eggs in each ramekin. Sprinkle pepper and salt over ramekin.

3.   In each ramekin, add 2 tablespoons of cream.

4.   Bake them in oven for 10 to 12 minutes. Sprinkle herbs to increase flavor.

Nutritional Information Per Serving:

271 total calories, 24 g fat, 471 mg cholesterol, 392 mg sodium, 13 g protein, 2 g carbohydrates, 1 g sugar, 0 g fiber, 2 mg iron and 74 mg calcium

Recipe 04: Cheesy Pancake

Cooking Time: 20 minutes
Servings: 18 to 20
Ingredients
- 2 cups cottage cheese (low-fat)
- 4 teaspoons baking powder
- 2 cups oats
- 2 cups egg whites
- 3 teaspoon sweetener
- 1 teaspoon vanilla

DIRECTIONS:
1. Blend two cup oats in a blender to make a fine powder. Add 2 cups of cottage cheese and egg whites in oats.
2. Add almost 4 teaspoons of baking powder and 3 teaspoons sweetener. Feel free to use honey instead of white sugar.
3. Mix in vanilla and blend it well. Take a nonstick frying pan and put it on the medium heat.
4. Pour mixture on the pan and let it cook for 4 to 5 minutes. Flip to other side and cook for another 2 to 3 minutes. Make almost 18 to 20 large pancakes.

Nutritional Information:
461 total calories, 65 g fat, 579 mg cholesterol, 1,868 mg sodium, 26 g protein, 8 g carbohydrate, 5 g sugar, and 2 g fiber

Recipe 05: Rainbow Vegetable Noodles

Cooking Time: 25 minutes
Servings: 2
Ingredients:
- 1 Zucchini
- 1 Summer Squash
- 1 Carrot
- 1 Sweet Potato
- 4 oz. Onion (Red)
- 3 Garlic Cloves
- 6 oz. Bell Peppers (Yellow, orange, and Red)
- 4 tablespoons butter
- Salt and Pepper As per taste

DIRECTIONS:

1.   Preheat oven to 400° F. Grease all the baking sheets with butter. Use a spiral slicer to make slices of zucchini, carrot, and sweet potato.

2.   Set these vegetables in a bowl similar to a rainbow. Combine all vegetables and sprinkle salt and pepper.

3.   Mix vegetables well and spread them on a baking sheet similar to noodles. Bake them for almost 20 minutes. Make sure to fold them after ten minutes.

Nutritional Ingredients Per Servings:
48 total calories, 1.5 g protein, 8 g carbs, 1 gram fat

Recipe 06: Cauliflower Salad

Cooking Time: 10 minutes
Servings: 2
Ingredients:
- 1 cauliflower (Head)
- 1 tablespoon olive oil
- 2 cucumbers
- 3 tablespoon dill, sliced
- ¼ cup olive oil
- ¼ cup lemon juice
- 2 tablespoons shredded lemon zest
- Salt & Pepper as per taste

Directions:
1.   Cut the florets of the cauliflower and throw the bottom stalk. Chop them into small pieces and bake the cauliflower in the microwave for almost 5 minutes to make them soft.
2.   Keep cauliflower aside to cool down. Chop the cucumber to make slices. Combine cauliflower and cucumber in a medium bowl. Sprinkle 1 tablespoon of olive oil and sprinkle salt and pepper.
3.   Mix in lemon zest and dill with olive oil and lemon juices. After mixing everything, season your favorite spices.

Nutritional Information per Serving:
114 total calories, 13 g fat, 0 g carbohydrates and 17 g protein.

Recipe 07: Avgolemono

Cooking Time: 10 to 20 minutes
Servings: 8
Ingredients:
- 4 cups chicken (cooked and shredded)
- Chicken broth (10 Cups)
- 3 eggs
- 1/3 cup lemon juice (fresh)
- 2 cups squash (cooked and shredded)
- 1/4 cup chopped parsley
- Salt as per your taste
- Pepper as per your taste
- Grated low-fat cheese

Directions:
1. Pour chicken broth in a saucepan along with shredded chicken and let them simmer. At boiling point, turn off stove and keep the pan aside.
2. Whisk eggs and lemon juice together in a bowl to create a frothy mixture. Mix 2 cups of hot stock slowly into the mixture and let them incorporate properly.
3. Avoid dumping the mixture because eggs may be scrambled. Pour the blend into the saucepan. Add in shredded squash in the soup and reheat it. Give it a boil and season with spices.
4. Add chopped parsley and cheese and serve hot.

Nutritional Information:
289 calories, 15g fat, 4g net carbs, and 33g protein

Recipe 08: Spaghetti Squash

Cooking Time: Over 1 hour
Servings: 4
Ingredients:
Crust
- 1 medium crushed spaghetti
- 1/2 tsp parsley
- 1/2 tsp onion
- 1/4 tsp salt

Filling:
- 1 chopped onion
- 3 cups chopped mushrooms
- 3/4 tsp black pepper, ground
- 5 crushed garlic cloves
- 2 eggs
- 2 cups kale
- 1 cup egg whites
- 1 cup cheese
- 2 tsp garlic powder
- 1 1/2 tsp dried thyme
- 1 cup cottage cheese
- 1/2 tsp salt
- Cooking spray

Directions:
1.   Preheat oven to 400 degrees F. Cut the squash in two halves and put them on the baking sheet. For squash, you can use parchment paper. Bake squash in a preheated oven for 30 minutes.
2.   Grease a frying pan and put it on heat. Sauté mushrooms for almost 5 minutes to get a golden brown color. Shift the mushrooms in the medium bowl and keep the frying pan again on medium flame after greasing it again.
3.   Fry garlic and onion for 2 minutes in a frying pan and add kale, salt, black pepper and basil as well to sauté them. Add these things in a bowl of mushroom and set it aside.
4.   Add garlic, onion, salt, and thyme to add in a medium bowl. Seed the squash with the help of a fork to make the crust. Transfer this to a deep pie dish and keep on a side.
5.   Whisk egg, add cheese, kale and garlic powder, basil, salt and pepper to make a perfect blend. Pour this blend into the crust and let the squash absorb the liquid. Bake it at 400 degrees F for 50 minutes. Leave it for 30 minutes after removing from oven and then cut into 8 slices.

Nutritional Information Per Serving:
Calories: 170.1, Fat: 6.4 g, Cholesterol: 61.5 mg, Sodium: 498.4 mg, Total Carbs: 14.5 g, Dietary Fiber: 3.3 g, Protein: 14.0 g

Recipe 09: Chocolate Milk

Cooking Time: 5 minutes
Servings: 2 servings
Ingredients:
- Almond milk (unsweetened): 16 ounces
- Low-carb sweetener: to taste
- Heavy cream: 4 ounces
- Whey chocolate powder: 1 scoop
- Crushed ice: ½ cup

Directions:
1.   Put all above mentioned ingredients in your blender and blend them well to make a smooth paste. Serve chilled.

Nutrition: Calories: 292, Fat: 25 grams, Carbs: 5 and Protein: 15 grams

Recipe 10: Hamburger Patties

Cooking Time: 35 minutes
Servings: 4
Ingredients:
- Ground beef: 1½ lbs
- Egg: 1
- Feta cheese: 3 oz.
- Salt: 1 teaspoon
- Black pepper: 1 pinch
- Chopped parsley: 2 oz.
- Olive oil: 1 tablespoon
- Butter: 1 tablespoon

Gravy
- Whipping cream (heavy): 5 fl. oz.
- Chopped parsley: 2 oz.
- Tomato paste: 1 tablespoon
- Pepper and salt as per taste

Directions:

2. Take a bowl and mix all ingredients well to make eight long or round patties.

3. Take a frying pan and heat olive oil and butter in this pan. Fry patties for almost 10 minutes to get a golden brown color.

4. Line a plate with paper towel and put patties on this towel to drain extra oil. Pour whipping cream and tomato sauce in one pan to let them boil together. Sprinkle parsley over the top and serve with patties.

Nutritional Information (1 serving):

253 calories, 12g fat, 23g protein, 13g carbohydrate

Recipe 11: Chocolate Bomb

Cooking Time: 2 hours
Servings: 25 pieces
Ingredients:
•2 oz Butter (you can choose anyone, but the cocoa butter is better for you)
•2 Tablespoons cocoa powder, without sugar
•2 Tablespoons Sweetener
•4 oz Macadamias (chopped)
•¼ cup coconut oil

Directions:
1.	Liquefy the cocoa butter in a cooking pan with water and now add cocoa in the pan. Now add sweetener and blend all the ingredients well. It is time to add macadamias and cream.
2.	Mix well and keep it on the flame. Once you get a smooth blend, it is time to add the molds in the candy cups made of papers and let them cool on a room temperature.
3.	You need to keep in the refrigerator to make them hard.

Nutritional Information:
Total calories 267, Carbs 3 grams, Protein 3 grams, and Fat 28 grams

Recipe 12: Cauliflower Rice

Cooking Time: 20 minutes
Servings: 4
Ingredients:
- Cauliflower head: 1¾ lbs
- Salt: ½ teaspoon
- Turmeric: ½ teaspoon
- Coconut oil: 3 oz.

Directions:
1.	Grate entire head of cauliflower with a grater and keep it aside.
2.	Melt coconut oil in one skillet and add cauliflower rice to cook on medium heat for almost 10 minutes.
3.	Add turmeric and salt in the rice while frying and put rice in one glass bowl. Cover this bowl with a plastic wrap to microwave them for almost 6 minutes.
4.	Mix coconut oil in hot rice and serve.

Nutritional Information:
113 calories, 7 g fat, 4.2 g protein, 11.1 g carbohydrate, 63 mg sodium, 0 mg cholesterol

Recipe 13: Blueberries Smoothie

Cooking Time: 10 minutes
Servings: 2
Ingredients:
•Almond milk, 1 cup
•2 tablespoons crushed almonds
•1/3 cup blueberries or any other berries of your choice
•One pinch salt
Directions:
1.   Take a food processor and make a blend of all these ingredients to make a delicious smoothie.
2.   Serve chilled by keeping in the refrigerator.
Nutritional Information:
835 total calories, 80 g fat, 30 g protein, 27 g carbohydrate and 2 g fiber.

Recipe 14: Low Carb Fruit Salad

Cooking Time: 10 minutes
Servings: 2
Ingredients:
- 1 cup berries (you can prepare a mixture by selecting your own favorite berries)
- 2 tablespoons mascarpone
- 1 sage leaf, small pieces
- 1/2 vanilla bean
- 1/2 tablespoons cream (heavy or whipping cream)

Directions:
1. Take a bowl to prepare a mixture of berries and cut sage.
2. In a separate bowl, make the mixture of rest of the ingredients and then keep in the microwave for 10 seconds.
3. Mix the blend of both the bowls and enjoy chilled.

Nutritional Information:
1.5 g fat, 4 g carbohydrate, and 2 g fibe

Recipe 15: Cinnamon Treat

Cooking Time: 40 minutes
Serving: 10
Ingredients
- Butter: 4 oz.
- Shredded coconut (unsweetened coconut): 1/3 cup
- Green cardamom: 1 pinch
- Vanilla extract: ¼ teaspoon
- Cinnamon: 2 pinches

Directions:
1. Put butter to your room temperature.
2. Carefully roast shredded coconut to make it light brown. It will enhance the flavor of your fat bombs.
3. Mix butter, shredded coconut (half) and all spices in one bowl. Make small balls with 2 teaspoons and roll each ball in the remaining shredded coconut.
4. Store them in freezer or refrigerator.

Nutrition Information for Each Cookie:
Calories 341, Fat, 31.9 g, Dietary Fiber 7.5 g, Protein 3.3 g, Carbohydrates 5.3 g

Fresh Juices to Improve Health of Gallbladder

Recipe 16: Beetroot, Carrot and Cucumber Juice

Cooking Time: 10 minutes
Serving: 1
Ingredients:
•1 Beetroot
•1 Carrot
•1 Cucumber
Directions:
1.	Beets have anti-inflammatory and antioxidant properties to promote healthy flow of bile.It contains betaine that is essential for healthy function of your liver. With the use of this juice, you can decrease the level of toxic homocysteine.
2.	Carrots have vitamin C to decrease calcium deposits. Moreover, cucumber contains water for soothing digestive system.
Nutritional Information:
Calories: 93 Sodium: 10mg Carbohydrates: 10g Protein: 3g Calcium: 61mg Iron: 0.6mg

Recipe 17: Lemonade Recipe

Cooking Time: 10 minutes
Serving: 1
Ingredients:
•1 cup water
•1 cup sugar substitute
•3 cups chilled water
•1 cup fresh lemon juice
Directions:
1.   In the first step, make syrup by adding sugar in water in a small pan and let it simmer. Mix well to dissolve sugar completely and turn off heat.
2.   Squeeze almost 6 to 8 lemons to get a cup of juice. Add this juice sugar syrup and add 3 cups of cold water. You can increase quantity of water and lemon juice as per your taste.
3.   Put this lemonade in the refrigerator and serve chilled.
Nutritional Information:
Calories: 83 Sodium: 15mg Carbohydrates: 20g Protein: 2g Calcium: 65mg Iron: 0.8mg

Recipe 18: Grape Fruit Juice with Apple Cider

Cooking Time: 10 minutes
Serving: 1
Ingredients:
•1 Grapefruit
•1 - 2 Teaspoon apple cider vinegar
Directions:
1.   Squeeze juice of a grapefruit and mix apple cider vinegar in this juice. This drink is healthy for everyone with its anti-cholesterol and antioxidant properties.
Nutritional Information:
Calories: 103 Sodium: 11 mg Carbohydrates: 23 g Protein: 1 g Calcium: 64 mg Iron: 0.8 mg

Recipe 19: Olive Oil and Lemon Juice

Cooking Time: 10 minutes
Serving: 1
Ingredients:
- 1 tablespoon olive oil
- 1 tablespoon lemon juice
- 1 tablespoon garlic paste

Directions:
1.   Mix everything in a glass of water and drink in the morning with an empty stomach. For the best results, use this juice consistently for one month.

Nutritional Information:
Calories: 93 Sodium: 21 mg Carbohydrates: 2 g Protein: 2 g Calcium: 60 mg Iron: 0.6 mg

Recipe 20: Lemonade with Lavender

Cooking Time: 10 minutes
Serving: 1
Ingredients:
- 1 rhubarb (1 pound), cut crosswise and clean
- 2 cups fresh water
- 3 tablespoons rosemary leaves
- 1 ½ cups sugar substitute
- ½ cup fresh lemon juice
- Carbonated water

Directions:
1. Put sugar, rosemary, water and rhubarb in a saucepan and put on medium-high heat. Let this blend boil and decrease to simmer to cook for 15 minutes.
2. Once rhubarb pieces are disintegrated, turn off the stove and strain this blend. Squeeze lemon juice in this drink as per your taste.
3. Mix in soda water (a quarter of soda water in ½ glass) with rosemary syrup. Serve chilled.

Nutritional Information:
Calories: 101, Sodium: 19 mg, Carbohydrates: 21 g, Protein: 5 g, Calcium: 50 mg, Iron: 0.7 mg

Recipe 21: Green Juice

Cooking Time: 10 minutes
Serving: 1
Ingredients:
- 2 green apples
- 4 celery stalks (remove leaves)
- 6 kale leaves
- 1 cucumber
- ½ peeled lemon
- 1-inch fresh ginger

Directions:

1.   Process apples, cucumber, celery, lemon, ginger and kale through your juice. Your juice is ready.

Nutritional Information:

Calories: 143.5, Sodium: 95.2 mg, Carbohydrates: 36 g, Protein: 4.2 g, Fat: 1.1 g

Recipe 22: Zinger Juice

Cooking Time: 10 minutes
Serving: 1
Ingredients:
•2 lemons without seeds (quartered, seeded and peeled)
•2 chopped carrots
•2 quartered apples
•2 chopped and trimmed beets
Directions:
1.   Press apples, carrots, beets and lemons through your juicer and serve in a glass.
Nutritional Information:
Calories: 158.1, Sodium: 118.3 mg, Carbohydrates: 45.6 g, Protein: 3.5 g, Fat: 0.9 g

Recipe 23: Watermelon Drink

Cooking Time: 10 minutes
Serving: 1
Ingredients:
- 4 cups seedless, cubed watermelon
- 1/3 cup of fresh lemon juice
- ¼ cup sugar substitute
- 1/8 teaspoon pink salt

Directions:
1. Put ice and watermelon in a blender. Blend them well and mix in salt, sugar, and lime juice. Once again blend to make a smooth drink.

Nutritional Information:
Calories: 29, Carbohydrates: 7.50 g, Protein: 0.42 g, Fiber: 0.40 g, Sugar: 5.42 g

Recipe 24: Blueberry Slush

Cooking Time: 10 minutes
Serving: 4
Ingredients:
•6 ounce fresh orange juice
•6 ounce water
•4 cubes of ice
•1 cup blueberries (fresh)
Directions:
1.   Put orange juice, blueberries, ice cubes and water in your blender. Blend everything well to make slushy juice.
2.   Pour it in a glass and serve chilled.
Nutritional Information:
Calories: 105.3, Carbohydrates: 25.6 g, Protein: 1.5 g, Calcium: 160 mg, Sodium: 3.9 mg

Delicious Recipes for Lunch

Recipe 25: Low-fat Pizza

Cooking Time: 30 minutes
Serving: 2
Ingredients
- Eggs: 4
- Shredded Cheese (Provolone or mozzarella): 6 oz.

Toppings
- Tomato Paste or sun-dried pesto: 4 tablespoons
- Oregano: 1 teaspoon
- Shredded cheese: 4 oz.
- Pepperoni: 2 oz.
- Olives: as per your needs

Directions:
1. Preheat an oven to almost 400°F.
2. Take a bowl and whisk eggs and cheese (6 ounces) in this bowl. Spread egg batter and cheese on the baking sheet lined with parchment paper and make two round circles or square pizzas. Now bake them for almost 15 minutes to make pizza crust golden.
3. Increase the temperature of the oven to almost 450°F.
4. Spread your tomato paste on this crust and sprinkle some oregano. Top with cheese, pepperoni, and olives.
5. Bake this pizza for almost ten minutes again to make pizza golden brown. You can serve it with salad.

Nutrition Information for Each Cookie:
Calories 335, Fat 27 g, Total Carbohydrate 3.2 g, Protein 18.2 g

Recipe 26: Chicken and Cheese

Cooking Time: 45 minutes

Serving: 4

Ingredients

- Chicken (breast or thighs): 1½ lbs
- Green or red pesto: 4 oz.
- Whipping cream (heavy): 1½ cups
- Pitted olives (green or black): ½ cup
- Diced feta cheese: ½ lb
- Chopped Garlic (fine): 1 clove
- Pepper and salt as per taste
- Olive oil or butter to fry

Directions:

1.   Preheat an oven to almost 400°F.
2.   Cut the fillets or thighs of chicken into small pieces. Sprinkle pepper and salt and fry them in butter or olive oil until golden.
3.   Mix heavy cream and pesto in one bowl.
4.   Put the pieces of fried chicken in one baking dish with feta cheese, garlic, and olives. Add pesto mixture and bake chicken in your oven for almost 20 to 30 minutes to get a beautiful color of this dish.
5.   Serve with leafy greens or baby spinach.

Nutrition Information:

Calories 210, Fat 11 g, Sodium 350 mg, Total Carbs 1 g, Protein 27 g

Recipe 27: Cauliflower Hash Browns

Cooking Time: 30 minutes
Serving: 4
Ingredients:
- Shredded cauliflower head: 1 lb
- Eggs: 3
- Grated onion: ½
- Salt: 1 teaspoon
- Pepper: 2 pinches
- Butter: 4 oz. for frying

Directions:

1.   Remove the leaves of cauliflower and shred cauliflower coarsely to get sufficient amount. You can save remaining cauliflower for another time.

2.   Take a bowl and mix shredded cauliflower with all other ingredients (except butter) in one bowl. Leave it for almost 10 minutes.

3.   Melt a good amount of butter in a frying pan and cook 3 to 4 pancakes. If you have a small pan, you can put a small amount of this blend to make one pancake. On a large pan, you can make 3 to 4 pancakes at a time.

4.   Place some mixture of grated cauliflower in your frying pan and make them flat with a spatula. Fry them for 4 to 5 minutes on every side on medium heat. Flip pancake to cook its other side.

5.   You can serve with spicy butter or mayonnaise.

Nutrition Information for Each Cookie:

Calories 95, Total Fat 7 g, Total Carbohydrates 3 g, Dietary Fiber 1.4 g, and Protein 5.6 g, cholesterol, 67 mg.

Recipe 28: Butter Spinach Soup

Cooking Time: 30 minutes
Serving: 6
Ingredients:
- 25g butter (low-fat)
- Spring onions chopped only 1 bunch
- 120-gram leek, chopped
- 85 g celery (about 2 small sticks), sliced
- 200 g potatoes (1 medium), peel it properly and divide into pieces
- ½ tsp black pepper (freshly ground)
- Make stock (made with two chicken or vegetable stock cubes)
- 2 bags spinach
- 150g half-fat cream

Directions:
1.	Take a large saucepan and let the butter melt, and now add onions, potatoes, celery and leek. Mix them well and put a lid on the pot to let them cook for 10 minutes.
2.	Keep stirring them and after 10 minutes, add stock in it. Now you will cook it for another 10 to 15 minutes until the potatoes and other vegetables become soft.
3.	In the end, add spinach and let it cook for a few minutes. You can blend the soup in a blender to make a smooth paste and mix the low-fat cream. Reheat the soup before serving it.

Nutritional Information:
192 calories, 6.5g protein, 13.1g carbs, 12.6g fat, 7.2g saturated fat, 5.4g fiber, 4.4g sugar, and 2g salt.

Recipe 29: Tomato and Onion Soup

Cooking Time: 30 minutes
Serving: 9
Ingredients:
- 1 medium onion, chopped
- Celery should be Properly chopped, 2 large stalks
- 4 cloves garlic, crushed
- 1 medium bell pepper (Red)
- 1 cup chopped carrot or pumpkin
- 1 full teaspoon of sweet paprika
- 3 teaspoons turmeric powder
- 1/2 teaspoon cinnamon
- 1 bay leaf
- Hot sauce to serve
- 1 cup tomato paste
- A green chard leaf and cut it into strips. (You can also use other green leafy vegetables like spinach or kale).
- Green beans almost 10 oz,
- Salt and pepper,
- 5 cups broth
- 1 tablespoon olive oil

Directions:
1. Add oil, onion and celery in a large pot. Cook for 5 to 10 minutes.
2. Put garlic into it and reduce heat to medium. Cook for a few minutes and add peppers and carrots in the pot. Cook for another minute before adding spices.
3. Now you will add tomato paste and stock. Cook for almost 15 minutes. Add beans and chard and let the soup boil for 5 minutes to cook beans. Now add shredded meat and serve hot with hot sauce.

Nutritional Information:
Servings, 9 cups of 6 grams, carbohydrate and 3 grams of fiber (9 grams total carbohydrate) and 53 calories

Recipe 30: Carrot Soup

Cooking Time: 30 minutes

Serving: 4 to 6

Ingredients:

- 1 tbsp vegetable oil
- 1 onion, sliced
- 1.2 lb vegetable stock (chicken stock can also be used)
- 1 potato, sliced
- 450g carrots chopped after peeling
- 1 tsp ground coriander
- Handful coriander (1/2 packet)

Directions:

1.   Take a large pan and add onion to let them fry for 5 minutes. Add coriander and potato to cook for 1 minute and add the carrots and broth to let them boil.

2.   At this point, reduce the heat and cover the pot for 20 minutes to make carrots soft. You can blend it in a blender to make everything smooth. Reheat while serving it.

Nutritional Information:

Calories 115, Protein 3g, Carbs 19g, Fat 4g, Saturates 1g, Fiber 5g, Sugar 12g, Salt 0.46g

Recipe 31: Chicken Soup

Cooking Time: 30+ minutes
Serving: 4 to 6
Ingredients:
- 1 small or 1/2 large onion, cut into pieces
- 2 stalks celery, cut into small pieces
- 1 large carrot, cut into small pieces
- 1 tablespoon olive oil
- 3 cloves garlic, crushed
- 1-quart chicken broth
- 1 cup chicken meat (cooked and chopped)
- 1/3 cup salsa
- 1/8 teaspoon black pepper
- 1/4 cup chopped leafy herbs like parsley, celery leaves, or oregano.
- Vegetables of your choice

Directions:
1.   Stir fry the onion and vegetable of your choice in a soup pot and then add garlic and fry for one minute.
2.   It is time to add broth, vegetables, and salt, but doesn't add green vegetables at the start. The green vegetables should be added at the end to avoid overcooking.
3.   Let the stock boil and cook on a medium heat to properly cook all vegetables. You may need more water to cook vegetables and then add low-fat butter, spices, and herbs and cook for one minute. Serve hot for better taste.

Nutritional Information:
5 grams of serving contains 5 grams carbohydrate and 1.5 grams of fiber, 11 grams of protein, and 92 calories.

Recipe 32: Fish Soup

Cooking Time: 30 minutes
Serving: 4 to 6
Ingredients:
- 8 ounces fresh sea bass fillets
- 6 ounces deveined shrimp
- 1/3 cup sliced onion
- 2 stalks sliced celery
- 1/2 teaspoon minced garlic
- 2 teaspoons olive oil
- 1 cup chicken broth (low salt)
- 1 14 diced tomatoes, without salt
- 1 teaspoon dried oregano, chopped
- 1/4 teaspoon salt
- 1/8 teaspoon freshly ground pepper
- 1 tablespoon fresh parsley

Directions:

1.   Defrost fish and shrimp and rinse properly. Let them dry on a white paper towel and then cut into pieces. The shrimp should be cut in lengthwise halves. You need to cook onion, garlic and celery in hot oil in a large saucepan and add broth.

2.   Let the mixture boil for 5 minutes and mix tomato sauce, oregano, and spices. Let them boil again and cover the pot for 5 minutes.

3.   Carefully mix fish and shrimp and let them boil on a low heat for 5 minutes to let the fish flake easily and shrimp opaque. Garnish parsley before serving hot.

Nutritional Information in Each Serving:

165 gram each serving, Fat 4 g, carb 12 g, 2 g fiber, 19 mg sodium

Recipe 33: Cauliflower Broth

Cooking Time: 30 minutes
Serving: 4 to 6
Ingredients:
- 8 slices bacon, sliced
- 1/2 small chopped onion
- 1 chopped celery stalk
- 2 garlic cloves, crushed
- Salt
- Black Pepper
- 4 cups chopped cauliflower
- 2 Tablespoons gluten-free flour
- 2 cups chicken chowder
- 2 cups milk
- Hot sauce as per needs
- 2-1/2 cups cheddar cheese
- 2 onions, chopped and green

Directions:
1. Mix chicken and flour together in a small bowl, and keep it on a side. Now cook the bacon in a large pot on a medium heat.
2. Transfer the bacon on towel paper with spoon having slots and keep this plate aside. You can cook celery, chopped onion, garlic and vegetable for 4 to 5 minutes. Sprinkle salt and pepper to cook them well.
3. Pour water in the pot, add water and let it cook for 5 to 7 minutes. Pour leftover chicken broth and milk in the pot and let it simmer.
4. Slowly mix the broth and chicken and flour, and let it cook again for 3 to 4 minutes. Turn off the flame and mix 2 cups of cheese and mix well to get a smooth texture.
5. Adjust the salt and pepper as per your taste and add hot sauce to enhance its flavor. Use grated cheese while serving it with onion and bacon.

Nutritional Information Per Serving:
Serves 8, 265 calories, 7 grams of carbs, and 15 grams of protein per serving

Recipe 34: Burger with Mushrooms

Cooking Time: 20 minutes
Serving: 4 to 6
Ingredients:
•Portabella Burgers (gluten-free)
•4 mushroom caps
•3 ½ tablespoons vinegar
•2 tablespoons olive oil
•2 sliced tomatoes
•2 sliced halloumi
•Sea salt
•Black Pepper
•1 handful of sage leaves

Directions:
1.   Let the grill heat over 450 degrees and in the meantime, wash mushroom caps. Take a shallow bowl and mix olive oil and vinegar.
2.   Mix the mushrooms in the blend and keep the mushroom on the grill for almost 5 minutes. Flip it 2 to 3 times and add halloumi for 2 minutes to the grill.
3.   Cook it on high heat and pour cheese over it. Season it with salt and pepper. Assemble the burger with tomato, mushroom, cheese and basil leaves. Serve hot with additional sauce.

Nutritional Information:
326 total calories, 15.1 g fat, 59 mg cholesterol, 476 mg sodium, 21.6 g protein, 24.9 g carbohydrate

Recipe 35: Turkey Burger

Servings: 5
Cooking Time: 50 minutes
Ingredients:
- Turkey mince: 500g
- Egg: 1
- Tomato pesto (sun-dried): 1 tablespoon
- Oregano: 1 tablespoon
- Pressed garlic: 2 cloves
- Black pepper: 2 teaspoons
- Oats: 40g
- Chopped basil: 1 handful
- Chopped onion: 1 small

Directions:
1.   Take a bowl and mix all ingredients for your turkey burgers in this bowl. Wet your both hands ad make five patties with this mixture.
2.   Bake these patties in your preheated oven at 400 °F for almost 30 to 40 minutes. Serve them with your favorite burger buns, salads, and sauce.

Nutritional Information:
Calories: 183.5, Sodium: 354.5 mg, Carbohydrates: 2.3 g, Protein: 20.9 g, Fat: 9.5 g

Recipe 36: Vegetarian Pie

Time: 30 minutes
Serves 4
Ingredients
- Chickpeas with water: 16oz (drained and rinsed)
- Frozen vegetables (mixed): 2 tea-cups (boil them in water)
- Lentils with water (drained and rinsed): 12oz
- Chopped tomatoes: 16oz (juice discarded and drained)
- Dry mixed herbs: 1 pinch
- Paprika: 1 teaspoon
- Couscous: 12oz
- Grated hard cheese: 2oz
- Ground black pepper: as per taste

Directions:
1. Put frozen vegetables in a pan filled with cold water and let it boil. You have to cook it for almost five minutes. Drain water and discard it.
2. In the meantime, put other ingredients except cheese and couscous in a pan and heat thoroughly. Now mix cooked vegetables. Put this blend in your ovenproof dish.
3. To cook couscous, follow the Directions written on its packet and sprinkle cooked couscous over the dish.
4. Sprinkle whole cheese over couscous and carefully grill to make it golden brown. Serve this dish with crusty bread.

Nutritional Information:
Calories: 380.2, Sodium: 873 mg, Carbohydrates: 40.8 g, Protein: 6.1 g, Fat: 21.1 g

Recipe 37: Onion Flan

Time: 30 minutes
Serves: 4
Ingredients
- Whole meal flour: 3oz
- Low fat spread: 1oz
- Salt: 1 pinch
- Vegetable fat (white): 1/2oz
- Cold water: 3 tablespoons
- Thinly sliced onion: 1 medium
- Grated cheddar cheese (reduced fat): 3oz
- Egg: 1
- Skimmed milk: 1/4 pint
- Dried mixed herbs: 1 Pinch
- Black pepper: as per taste
- Flan tin: 7"

Directions:
1.   Preheat your oven to 350°F and keep gas mark at 4.
2.   Rub vegetable fat and low-fat spread in flour to make fine breadcrumbs. Add sufficient cold water so that you can make a firm dough.
3.   Thinly roll out and put in your flat tin. Prick its base and carefully organize onion on the foundation of flan case.
4.   Whisk herbs, milk, egg, and cheese together and season with some black pepper as per taste. Pour this blend over onion.
5.   Bake for almost 45 minutes. Serve cold or hot with salad and grilled/boiled potatoes. You can also serve with crusty bread.

Nutritional Information:
Calories: 617.8, Sodium: 3335.7 mg, Carbohydrates: 39.5 g, Protein: 29.7 g, Iron: 3.4 mg, Fat: 35.9 g

Recipe 38: Stir-fry Tofu

Time: 25 minutes
Serves: 2
Ingredients

- Plain tofu: 8oz (drained)
- Olive oil: 1 tablespoon
- Crushed garlic: 1 clove
- Peeled & finely chopped root ginger: 2 inches
- Head broccoli (chop in small florets): 1/2 small
- Carrot (chop into matchstick strips): 1
- Trimmed and chopped spring onions: 3 (cut into strips)
- Egg noodles: 4oz
- Soy sauce (reduced salt): 1 tablespoon
- Honey: 1 tablespoon
- Sesame oil: 1 teaspoon
- Ground black pepper: as per taste

Directions:

1. Cut tofu into small cubes and put these cubes in one bowl with garlic, ginger and olive oil. Toss well to mix and set it aside.
2. To cook noodles, follow the Directions given on the pack of noodles and drain. Use colder water to rinse noodles, drain and toss in some seasoned oil to keep noodles separated.
3. Boil carrots and broccoli in sufficient unsalted water for almost 5 minutes, drain water and use cold water to rinse.
4. Heat one non-stick frying pan or wok and add marinated tofu. Stir-fry tofu for almost 2 to 3 minutes.
5. Stir in water (1 tablespoon), broccoli and carrot. Cover non-stick pan with one lid and steam for almost 4 to 5 minutes to cook tofu. Mix in spring onions for last minute.
6. Take one bowl and mix honey and Soy sauce (reduced salt). Add noodles to pan with soy blend. Toss well to make everything piping hot.
7. Season with some black pepper as per your taste and serve instantly.

Nutritional Information:
Calories: 350.5, Sodium: 678.5 mg, Carbohydrates: 31.2 g, Protein: 12.3 g, Calcium: 117.9 mg, Iron: 1.5 mg, Fat: 24.4 g

Recipe 39: Tomato Rice

Time: 30 minutes
Serves: 2
Ingredients
- Long grain white or brown rice: 4oz
- Chopped and peeled tomato: 1 medium
- Minced chilli pepper: 1
- Vegetable oil: 2 teaspoons
- Stock cube (reduced salt): 1/2
- Minced garlic: 1 clove
- Chopped onion: 1 medium

Directions:
1.   Boil rice for almost 5 minutes, drain and use cold water to rinse rise and remove extra starch. Boil rice again in 1/3 pint of chilled water with a stock cube.
2.   Mix in hot chili, vegetable oil, and tomato. Cook for almost 30 to 40 minutes to let the water absorbed.
3.   Serve with side salad and grilled potatoes.

Nutritional Information:
Calories: 292.2, Sodium: 1817.4 mg, Carbohydrates: 52.8 g, Protein: 8.6 g, Calcium: 65.5 mg, Iron: 3.1 mg, Fat: 5.6 g

Recipe 40: Mint Couscous

Time: 20 minutes
Serves: 4
Ingredients
- Couscous: 8oz
- Water: 1 pint
- Chopped and fresh mint: 3 tablespoons
- Olive oil: 2 teaspoons

Directions:

1.   Boil water in a pan. Remove pan from heat and add couscous in boiled water. Mix briefly and use a lid to cover pan. Keep it aside for almost 5 minutes and fluff up couscous with one fork.

2.   Drizzle with some oil and add chopped mint. Use black pepper for seasoning and serve with fish or meat, or a vegan dish.

Nutritional Information:
Calories: 306, Sodium: 163.7 mg, Carbohydrates: 53.7 g, Protein: 10.9 g, Calcium: 54.4 mg, Iron: 3.1 mg, Fat: 5.3 g

Recipe 41: Cheesy Caprese

Time: 15 minutes
Servings: 6
Ingredients:
- Sliced ripe tomatoes: 4 large
- Mozzarella cheese (fresh): 1 pound (1/4 inch thick)
- Basil leaves (fresh): 1/3 cup (1/4 inch thick)
- Olive oil (extra virgin): 3 tablespoons
- Salt (with low sodium): as per taste
- Ground black pepper: as per taste

Directions:
1.   Take a platter and overlap tomato slices, basil leaves and slices of mozzarella cheese.
2.   Drizzle with some olive oil and season with pepper and salt. Serve.

Nutritional Information:
Calories: 580.1, Sodium: 330.9 mg, Carbohydrates: 34.8 g, Protein: 22 g, Calcium: 692.4 mg, Iron: 1.9 mg, Fat: 38.8 g

Recipe 42: Mango Salsa

Time: 20 minutes

Servings: 8

Ingredients:

- Pitted, peeled and diced avocado: 1
- Lime: 1 (juiced)
- Seeded, peeled and diced mango: 1
- Chopped red onion: 1 small
- Chopped and seeded habanero pepper: 1
- Chopped cilantro: 1 tablespoon
- Salt: to taste

Directions:

1. Put avocado in your serving bowl and mix it with lime juice.
2. Stir in salt, cilantro, habanero pepper, onion and mango.

Nutritional Information:

Calories: 21, Sodium: 1.4 mg, Carbohydrates: 5.4 g, Protein: 0.3 g, Calcium: 5.6 mg, Iron: 0.1 mg, Fat: 0.1 g

Recipe 43: Roasted Ladyfinger

Time: 20 minutes
Servings: 3
Ingredients:
- Kosher salt: 2 teaspoons or as per taste
- Okra pods: 18 (1/3-inch slices)
- Black pepper: 2 teaspoon
- Olive oil: 1 tablespoon

Directions:
1.   Preheat oven to 425°F.
2.   Arrange slices of okra in a layer on a cookie sheet lined with a foil. Drizzle with some olive oil and sprinkle with pepper and salt.
3.   Bake in your preheated oven for 10 – 15 minutes.

Nutritional Information:
Calories: 98, Sodium: 8 mg, Carbohydrates: 9 g, Protein: 2 g, Calcium: 51 mg, Iron: 0.7 mg, Fat: 5 g

Recipe 45: Healthy Pasta

Time: 30 minutes
Servings: 6
Ingredients:
- Uncooked pasta: 12 ounces
- Frozen vegetables (mixed): 12 ounces
- Low-sodium vegetable broth: 14 ounces
- All-purpose flour: 2 tablespoons
- Half-and-half creamer: ¼ cup
- Garlic powder: ¼ teaspoon
- Parmesan cheese (grated): ¼ cup

Directions:
1.   Cook pasta in a separate pot as per the directions of package. Make sure to omit salt and drain. Boil vegetables without extra salt. Drain and keep aside.
2.   Pour vegetable broth in one stockpot and cook it on medium-low heat. Stir in flour to vegetable broth and whisk vigorously to decrease the chances of clumps.
3.   Mix in garlic powder and half-and-half. Simmer this blend on low flame for 5 – 10 minutes until mixture thickens slightly. Mix occasionally while bubbling.
4.   Mix cooked pasta and vegetables in bubbling mixture and cook until it heated through.
5.   Now sprinkle with some parmesan cheese. Serve hot.

Nutritional Information:
Calories: 189.9, Sodium: 336.3 mg, Carbohydrates: 27.1 g, Protein: 4.7 g, Calcium: 21.6 mg, Iron: 1.4 mg, Fat: 7.4 g

Recipe 46: Egg Salad with Olives

Cooking Time: 20 minutes
Servings: 2
Ingredients:
Dressing
- Rapeseed oil: 2 tablespoons
- Lemon Juice: 1 lemon
- Balsamic vinegar: 1 teaspoon
- Grated garlic: 1 clove
- Chopped Basil: ⅓ cup
- Back kalamata olives (chopped and pitted): 3

Salad
- Eggs: 2
- Potatoes (sliced): 1 ½ cup
- Green beans: 1 cup
- Chopped red onion: ½
- Cherry tomatoes (halved): 14
- Romaine lettuce (torn leaves to make bite-sized pieces): 6
- Kalamata olive (pitted, halved and rinsed): 6

Directions:

1.   Take a bowl and mix all dressing ingredients in this bowl and stir in 1 tablespoon water. Keep it aside.

2.   Boil potatoes for almost seven minutes and add beans in potatoes to boil them again for five minutes to tender both ingredients. Boil eggs for approximately 8 minutes and shell. Split all eggs diagonally. Drain potatoes and beans, peel potatoes and chop them.

3.   Take one bowl and toss potatoes, beans, and remaining salad ingredients (except eggs) in this bowl. Stir in half dressing and arrange eggs on the top. Drizzle remaining dressing over eggs and serve this salad.

Nutritional Information:
Calories: 343.8, Sodium: 350.6 mg, Carbohydrates: 2.3 g, Protein: 13 g, Calcium: 60.6 mg, Iron: 2 mg, Fat: 31.9 g

Recipe 47: Potato Salad

Cooking Time: 10 minutes
Servings: 4
Ingredients:
- Boiled Potatoes (chopped): 4
- Olive oil: 2 tablespoons
- Lemon juice: ½ lemon
- Chopped parsley: 1 handful
- Boiled eggs: 2
- Wild rocket: 1 cup
- Diced cucumber: 1

Direction:
1. Take one bowl and toss boiled potatoes with parsley, lemon juice and olive oil in this bowl.
2. Stir in chopped boiled eggs, mix rocket leaves, and diced cucumber to serve.

Nutritional Information:
Calories: 338.8, Sodium: 538.1 mg, Carbohydrates: 20.4 g, Protein: 4.1 g, Calcium: 24.6 mg, Iron: 1.2 mg, Fat: 27.6 g

Recipe 48: Gherkins Salad

Cooking Time: 25 minutes
Servings: 4
Ingredients:
- Gherkins: 780 g
- Cucumber: 1
- Red Pepper: 1
- Green pepper: 1
- Yellow pepper: 1
- Red onion: 1
- Chili sauce: 100 ml
- Veg pickle: 8 teaspoon

Direction:
1. Wash vegetables and keep them aside.
2. Dice cucumber into tiny pieces.
3. Dice green, red and yellow pepper.
4. Chop red onion.
5. Put all vegetables in a bowl along with chili sauce and pickle.
6. You can keep in the fridge for 30 minutes and serve.

Nutritional Information:
Calories: 347.3, Sodium: 355.7 mg, Carbohydrates: 3 g, Protein: 13.1 g, Calcium: 62.7 mg, Iron: 2.1 mg, Fat: 31.9 g

Recipe 49: Watercress Sandwich

Cooking Time: 20 minutes
Servings: 4
Ingredients:
- Hard-boiled Eggs: 8 large
- Chopped scallions: 4
- Greek Yogurt or Sour cream (nonfat): 3 tablespoons
- Mayonnaise (reduced-fat): 1 tablespoon
- Grainy mustard: 1 tablespoon
- Ground black pepper and salt: as per taste
- Stemmed and washed watercress: ¾ cup
- Pumpernickel bread: 8 slices

Directions:
1.   In the first step, put eggs in one saucepan (in one layer) and cover all eggs with cold water. Place this pan on medium heat to let this water boil and decrease flame to low. Cook eggs at low temperature for almost ten minutes.
2.   Turn off heat and drain hot water. Leave these boiled eggs under a running stream of water for a few moments to let them cool. Peel them and cut each egg from middle to make two pieces.
3.   Scoop out yolks of all eggs, put two yolks in one small bowl, and reserve remaining yolks for next use. Chop all egg whites and keep them aside. Use a fork to mash yolks and mix in yogurt or sour cream, mustard, and mayonnaise. Mix in scallion and egg whites and season with pepper and salt.
4.   Arrange watercress leaves on four bread slices and top each slice with egg salad. Cover all slices with remaining slices of bread and serve with your favorite sauce.

Nutritional Information:
Calories: 157.7, Sodium: 317.2 mg, Carbohydrates: 13.3 g, Protein: 4.2 g, Calcium: 44.7 mg, Iron: 0.8 mg, Fat: 10.1 g

Recipe 50: Egg and Tomato Salad

Cooking Time: 1
Servings: 30 Minutes
Ingredients:
- Eggs: 2
- Banana slices: ½ cup
- Vanilla yogurt (low-fat): 2 tablespoons
- Diced celery: 2 tablespoons
- Low-fat mayonnaise: 1 tablespoon
- Raw or cooked broccoli florets: 2/3 cup
- Dijon mustard: 2 teaspoons
- Scallion greens (minced): 1 teaspoon
- Cherry tomatoes: 6
- Pumpernickel bread (cocktail-size): 3 slices
- Unsalted pistachios (shelled): 1 tablespoon
- Ground pepper: as per taste
- Bibb or Boston lettuce: 2 leaves
- Chocolate chips (bittersweet): 1 tablespoon
- Blueberries: ½ cup

Direction:

1.   In the first step, put eggs in one saucepan (in one layer) and cover all eggs with cold water. Place this pan on medium heat to let this water boil and decrease flame to low. Cook eggs at low temperature for almost ten minutes. Turn off heat and drain hot water. Leave these boiled eggs under a running stream of water for a few moments to let them cool. Peel them and cut each egg from middle to make two pieces.

2.   Take one big bowl and mash eggs in this bowl with one fork. Mix in pepper, scallion greens, mustard, mayonnaise and celery. Mix them well to combine all ingredients. Line your one container with green lettuce leaves and fill egg salad to this container. For better taste, you can keep this container in the fridge for almost two days after covering it.

3.   Take another container to combine yogurt, banana and blueberries. Arrange tomatoes and broccoli in another container.

4.   Put bread slices in the 4th container. Snuggle bread in one dip-size container and add chocolate chips and pistachios in this container. Serve this delicious box for lunch.

Nutritional Information:
Calories: 89, Sodium: 65 mg, Carbohydrates: 3 g, Protein: 6 g, Calcium: 25 mg, Iron: 0.6 mg, Fat: 1 g

Delicious Gallbladder Dinner Recipes
Recipe 51: Zucchini

Total Time: 40 minutes
Servings: 6
Ingredients:
- Zucchinis (Sliced): 4
- Salt: 1 teaspoon
- Vegetable oil: ½ cup
- Baking mix (buttermilk): 1 cup
- Beaten eggs: 4
- Chopped onion: ½ cup
- Parmesan cheese (grated): ½ cup

Directions:
1. Preheat your oven to almost 350 °F.
2. Combine eggs, oil, salt, parmesan cheese, onion, buttermilk mix, and zucchini in one mixing bowl.
3. Spread this mixture on a greased (9x13-inch) baking pan. Bake for almost 30 minutes and serve warm.

Nutritional Information:
Calories: 151, Sodium: 792.9 mg, Carbohydrates: 12.1 g, Protein: 6.5 g, Calcium: 91.9 mg, Iron: 1.3 mg, Fat: 9.8 g

Recipe 52: Creamy Spinach

Total Time: 20 minutes
Servings: 6
Ingredients:
- Butter: 1 tablespoon
- Chopped spinach: 10-ounce can
- Garlic salt: as per taste
- Condensed mushroom cream soup: 10.75 ounces

Directions:
1. Prepare spinach as per the directions and drain well. If you have fresh spinach, you can boil it and squeeze well to remove water.
2. Take one saucepan and combine butter, mushroom soup and spinach in this pan. Cook over medium flame and let it boil.
3. Season with some garlic salt and cook well to get a creamy texture. Serve warm.

Nutritional Information:
Calories: 96.2, Sodium: 441 mg, Carbohydrates: 6.9 g, Protein: 3 g, Calcium: 96.9 mg, Iron: 1.4 mg, Fat: 7 g

Recipe 53: Buttery Carrots

Total Time: 20 minutes
Servings: 4
Ingredients:
- Baby carrots: 1 pound
- Butter: 2 tablespoons
- Salt: 1 pinch
- Orange juice: ¼ cup
- Brown sugar: 3 tablespoons

Directions:
1. Put carrots in one shallow pan and cover this pan with water. Boil carrots until tender and drain them.
2. Add carrots in the pan again and drizzle orange juice on carrots. Mix it well and simmer on medium flame for almost five minutes.
3. Stir in salt, butter, and brown sugar. Heat sugar and butter to melt and serve warm.

Nutritional Information:
Calories: 135.8, Sodium: 131.3 mg, Carbohydrates: 20.8 g, Protein: 0.9 g, Calcium: 47.7 mg, Iron: 1.1 mg, Fat: 5.9 g

Recipe 54: Tuna Patties

Total Time: 30 minutes
Servings: 4
Ingredients:
- Cooking spray: as per your need
- Garlic salt: ¾ teaspoon
- Drained tuna (canned tuna with water): 6 ounce
- Egg: 1
- Diced tomatoes: ½ cup
- Black pepper (ground): 1 teaspoon
- Minced onion: ¼ cup
- Bread crumbs (dry): ½ cup

Directions:
1.   Preheat your oven to almost 375 °F. Grease one baking sheet with your cooking spray.
2.   Take one bowl and mix diced tomatoes, black pepper, garlic salt, bread crumbs, egg and tuna in this bowl. Mix them well and make four patties with this mixture.
3.   Put these patties on your greased baking sheet and bake in your preheated oven for almost ten minutes.
4.   Turn their sides and bake again for 8 to 10 minutes to make them crisp and golden brown.

Nutritional Information:
Calories: 353.1, Sodium: 779 mg, Carbohydrates: 36.6 g, Protein: 16.4 g, Calcium: 113.3 mg, Iron: 3.2 mg, Fat: 15.6 g

Recipe 55: Tilapia with Cheese

Total Time: 15 minutes
Servings: 8
Ingredients:
- Parmesan cheese: ½ cup
- Black pepper (ground): ¼ teaspoon
- Onion powder: 1/8 teaspoon
- Softened butter: ¼ cup
- Celery salt: 1/8 teaspoon
- Mayonnaise: 3 tablespoons
- Tilapia fillets: 2 pounds
- Lemon juice: 2 tablespoons
- Dried basil: ¼ teaspoon

Directions:
1.   Preheat the broiler of your oven and grease one broiling pan. You can also line it with an aluminum foil.
2.   Mix lemon juice, mayonnaise, butter, and parmesan cheese together in one small bowl. Season with celery salt, onion powder, pepper, and dry basil, mix well and keep this mixture aside.
3.   Arrange fish fillets in one single layer on your greased pan and broil for almost 2 – 3 minutes by keeping it 2 – 3 inches from heat. Flip all fillets and broil for two minutes again. Remove fillets and cover them with cheese mixture.
4.   Broil for two minutes again to make the topping brown. If the fish is easy to flake, it is ready to serve. There is no need to overcook fish.

Nutritional Information:
Calories: 224.4, Sodium: 220.5 mg, Carbohydrates: 0.8 g, Protein: 25.4 g, Calcium: 94.8 mg, Iron: 0.3 mg, Fat: 12.8 g

Recipe 56: Crispy Chicken

Total Time: 45 minutes
Servings: 6
Ingredients:
- Saltine crackers: 30
- Black pepper (ground): ½ teaspoon
- Egg: 1
- All-purpose flour: 2 tablespoons
- Chicken (boneless and skinless): 6 breast (halves)
- Vegetable oil: 2 cups
- Seasoned salt: 1 teaspoon
- Potato flakes (dry): 2 tablespoons

Directions:

1.   Put crackers in a plastic bag (resealable) and seal this bag to crush crackers with your rolling pin. Make coarse crumbs and combine with potatoes, seasoned salt, potato flakes, pepper, and salt. Mix them well.

2.   Whisk eggs in a bowl (one at a time) and dredge all chicken pieces in whisked eggs. Put all chicken pieces in the plastic bag of crumb mixture and seal this bag. Shake well to coat all chicken pieces.

3.   Heat oil in a saucepan or deep-fryer to almost 350 °F. Fry all chicken pieces and turn frequently, until golden brown and crisp. It may take approximately 15 – 20 minutes. Serve warm with tomato sauce.

Nutritional Information:
Calories: 623.1, Sodium: 107.7 mg, Carbohydrates: 21.9 g, Protein: 38.9 g, Calcium:25.2 mg, Iron: 2.8 mg, Fat: 41.3 g

Recipe 57: Healthy Chicken Nuggets

Total Time: 40 minutes
Servings: 4
Ingredients:
- Chicken (skinless and boneless): 4 breasts
- Seasoned bread crumbs (dried): ½ cup
- Wheat germ: ½ cup
- Whisked eggs: 2
- Dried basil: 1 teaspoon
- Water: 1 tablespoon
- Black pepper (ground): 1 teaspoon
- Chopped parsley: 1 teaspoon
- Dried thyme: ½ teaspoon
- Crushed Pepper flakes (red): 1 pinch
- Vegetable oil: 1 tablespoon

Directions:
1. Preheat your oven to almost 425 °F. Spray one baking sheet with a cooking spray.
2. Trim off any fat from your chicken pieces and cut into cubes (1-inch).
3. Whisk eggs and water in one bowl and add chicken in this bowl. Keep it aside.
4. Combine pepper, basil, wheat germ, bread crumbs, red pepper, thyme and parsley in one bowl. Mix in oil with one fork and mix them well to distribute equally. Pour seasoning blend in one releasable plastic bag, add chicken pieces and toss them well to coat.
5. Put coated pieces of chicken on your greased baking sheet and bake in your preheated oven for almost ten minutes. Turn all pieces and bake for an extra five minutes. Serve warm with tomato sauce.

Nutritional Information:
Calories: 308.4, Sodium: 989 mg, Carbohydrates: 14.6 g, Protein: 19.3 g, Calcium: 142 mg, Iron: 2.1 mg, Fat: 19.1 g

Recipe 58: Tangy Fillets with Potato Flakes

Total Time: 20 minutes
Servings: 4
Ingredients:
- Egg: 1
- Instant Potato flakes (mashed): 1 ½ cups
- Frying oil: ¼ cup
- Yellow mustard (prepared): 2 tablespoons
- 4 Fillets sole: 6 ounces
- Salt: ½ teaspoon

Directions:
1.   Take one shallow dish and whisk salt, mustard, and egg together. Keep it aside. Put your potato flakes in a separate shallow dish.
2.   Heat frying oil in your heavy skillet over medium heat.
3.   Dip your fish fillets in whisked egg mixture and dredge them into potato flakes. Make sure to coat each fillet thoroughly. If you want extra crispy flavor, dip in the egg mixture and potato flakes again.
4.   Fry these fillets in hot oil for almost 3 – 4 minutes on every side to make them golden brown. Serve warm with tomato sauce.

Nutritional Information:
Calories: 198.5, Sodium: 714.9 mg, Carbohydrates: 1.7 g, Protein: 16.6 g, Calcium: 16.9 mg, Iron: 1.1 mg, Fat: 12.5 g

Recipe 59: Chicken Balls with Italian Taste

Total Time: 40 minutes
Servings: 5
Ingredients:
- Ground chicken: 1 pound
- Italian seasoning: 1 tablespoon
- Garlic powder: 1 tablespoon
- Beaten eggs: 2
- Vegetable oil: 1 ½ tablespoons
- Garlic Cream cheese (light and roasted): ¼ cup
- Salt: 1 teaspoon
- Parmesan cheese (grated):¼ cup
- Black pepper (ground): 1 teaspoon
- Bread crumbs (dry): 1 tablespoon
- Crushed Pepper flakes (red): 1 teaspoon

Directions:
1. Preheat your oven to almost 450°F. Line one rimmed baking pan/sheet with an aluminum foil and grease with a cooking spray.
2. Combine pepper, salt, vegetable oil, garlic powder, Italian seasoning, pepper flakes, bread crumbs, parmesan cheese, cream cheese, eggs and chicken in one bowl. Form almost 20 meatballs with this mixture and put on one greased pan.
3. Bake in the middle of your preheated oven for almost 17 – 18 minutes to clear all juice. Use an instant thermometer to check temperature and it should be almost 165 °F.

Nutritional Information:
Calories: 175.4, Sodium: 299 mg, Carbohydrates: 3.2 g, Protein: g, Fat: 8.1 g

Recipe 60: Egg Noodles with Tuna and Peas

Total Time: 1 hour
Servings: 6
Ingredients:
- Egg noodles: 8 ounces
- Milk: 1 cup
- Cheddar cheese (shredded): 1 cup
- Butter: 2 tablespoons
- Tuna (drained): 6-ounce can
- All-purpose flour: 2 tablespoons
- Salt: 1 teaspoon
- Drained peas: 15-ounce

Directions:
1.   Preheat an oven to almost 350 °F. Coat your 2-quart casserole dish with nonstick cooking spray.
2.   Boil noodles in a pot filled with salted boiling water to al dente and drain well.
3.   Take one saucepan and combine salt, butter and flour in this pan. Stir well and cook on medium heat to melt butter and combined with other ingredients. Stir in milk and whisk well to make this sauce thick (you have to wait until it boils). Stir cheese to this blend and whisk well to equally blend this mixture. Mix in noodles, tuna and peas.
4.   Spread this mixture in a greased dish and bake in your preheated oven for almost 30 minutes.

Nutritional Information:
Calories: 345.5, Sodium: 721 mg, Carbohydrates: 34.2 g, Protein: 19.3 g, mg, Fat: 14.6 g

Recipe 61: Chicken Skewers with Brown Sugar

Total Time: 2 hours 30 minutes
Servings: 8
Ingredients:
- Soy sauce: 3 tablespoons
- Garlic powder: ¼ teaspoon
- Chicken (skinless and boneless): 8 breast halves (cut into 2-inch pieces)
- Brown sugar: 3 tablespoons
- Pineapple chunks (drained): 20 ounces
- Sherry: 2 tablespoons
- Skewers: as per your needs
- Sesame oil: 1 tablespoon
- Ground ginger: ¼ teaspoon

Directions:
1. Mix garlic powder, ginger, sesame oil, sherry, brown sugar and soy sauce in one shallow dish.
2. Mix in the pineapples and chicken pieces and coat well in this marinade. Cover this dish and put in your refrigerator for two hours or even more as per your available time.
3. Preheated one grill to almost medium heat.
4. Lightly oil your grill grate. Thread pineapple and chicken pieces alternately on your skewers.
5. Grill for approximately 15 – 20 minutes and turn occasionally. Let the juices dry and tender chicken. Serve warm with tomato sauce.

Nutritional Information:
Calories: 256, Sodium: 761.8 mg, Carbohydrates: 29.6 g, Protein: 25.6 g, Iron: 1.3 mg, Fat: 3.2 g

Recipe 62: Fruity Dessert with Cinnamon

Total Time: 45 minutes
Servings: 10
Ingredients:
- Brown sugar: 1 tablespoon
- Kiwis (peeled & died): 2
- Fruit preserves (choose your favorite flavor): 3 tablespoons
- Golden apples (peeled, cored & diced): 2
- Flour tortillas (10-inch): 10
- Raspberries: 8 ounces
- Cooking spray: butter flavored
- Strawberries: 1 pound
- Cinnamon sugar: 2 tablespoons
- White sugar: 2 tablespoons

Directions:
1.   Mix fruit preserves, brown sugar, white sugar, strawberries, raspberries, golden apples and kiwis in one mixing bowl. Cover this bowl and put in your fridge for almost 15 minutes.
2.   Preheat your oven to almost 350 °F.
3.   Coat one side of every tortilla with cooking spray and cut into wedges. Arrange them in one layer on your greased baking sheet (you can bake in batches). Sprinkle desired amount of cinnamon sugar on these wedges and spray again with butter-flavored cooking spray.
4.   Bake in your preheated oven for almost 8 – 10 minutes. Replicate this procedure with all tortilla wedges and let them cool for almost 15 minutes. Serve with chilled mixture of fruits.

Nutritional Information:
Calories: 70, Sodium: 86.2 mg, Carbohydrates: 12.5 g, Protein: 1.3 g, Iron: 0.5 mg, Fat: 1.8

Recipe 63: Fruity Dinner to Stay Healthy

Total Time: 5 minutes
Servings: 4
Ingredients:
- Ice cubes: 1 cup
- Sliced kiwi: 1
- Orange juice: ½ cup (fresh)
- Peach yogurt: 8 ounces
- Blueberries: ½ cup
- Strawberries: 1 cup
- Chopped banana (peeled): 1

Directions:
1.   Combine yogurt and all fruits in one blender and blend them for almost 2 – 3 minutes. Add ice to this mixture and blend again for two minutes.
2.   Pour into glasses and serve this chilled smoothie. You can add some nuts and almond milk in this smooth to replace yogurt.

Nutritional Information:
Calories: 315, Sodium: 190.8 mg, Carbohydrates: 43.4 g, Protein: 23.8 g, Calcium: 386.4 mg, Iron: 1.5 mg, Fat: 5.4 g

Recipe 64: Chocolate Dinner Side

Total Time: 5 minutes
Servings: 1
Ingredients:
- Banana: 1
- Almond milk: 1 cup
- Crushed ice: 1 cup
- Chocolate syrup: 1 tablespoon
- Chocolate chips (semisweet): 2 tablespoons
- Mango pulp: ½ cup
- Crushed almonds: 2 tablespoons

Directions:
1.   Combine mango pulp, almond milk and banana in a blender and process these ingredients.
2.   Add almonds, chocolate chips and chocolate syrup in this blend and process them again. Finally add ice and process all ingredients for almost 2 minutes.
3.   Pour into glasses and serve chilled. You can top with smoothie with low-fat cream.

Nutritional Information:
Calories: 341, Sodium: 90 mg, Carbohydrates: 78.9 g, Protein: 5.5 g, Calcium: 53.1 mg, Iron: 2.4 mg, Fat: 1.8 g

Recipe 65: Salmon and Herbs

Total Time: 30 minutes

Servings: 2

Ingredients:

- Salmon fillets (boneless): 6 ounces
- Olive oil: 1 teaspoon
- Parmesan cheese (grated): 2 tablespoons
- Dried basil: 1 tablespoon
- Sliced tomato: 1

Directions:

1.   Preheat your oven to almost 375 °F. Line one baking sheet with aluminum foil and grease with cooking spray.

2.   Put salmon fillets on this greased foil and sprinkle with some basil. Top with tomato slices and drizzle with oil. Sprinkle some parmesan cheese over salmon.

3.   Bake in your preheated oven for almost 20 minutes to make salmon opaque and easy to flake. Let the cheese equally brown. Serve with your favorite spicy sauce.

Nutritional Information:

Calories: 315.5, Sodium: 108.5 mg, Carbohydrates: 6.9 g, Protein: 23.2 g, Calcium: 103.2 mg, Iron: 1.8 mg, Fat: 21.9 g

Recipe 66: Chicken with Walnut Cheese

Total Time: 55 minutes
Servings: 4
Ingredients:
- Chicken (skinless and boneless): 2 breasts (horizontally halved)
- Walnut halves: 6 ounces
- Bacon: 8 slices
- Blue cheese (crumbled) 8 ounces
- Spices: as per taste

Directions:
1.   Preheat your oven to almost 350 °F.
2.   Pound chicken breast to make them equally thick (1/4-inch). Top each chicken breast with walnuts and blue cheese and roll chicken over filling.
3.   Put two bacon slices on your work surface (side-by-side) and put each chicken roll at the end of each bacon slice. Roll bacon around your chicken rolls and use a toothpick to secure. Replicate this procedure with remaining bacon and chicken rolls.
4.   Heat one skillet over medium flame and cook wrapped rolls in a hot skillet for almost 4 – 5 minutes for each side to make them crispy and brown.
5.   Sprinkle some spices over rolls as per your needs and transfer in your preheated oven. Bake for almost 25 – 35 minutes to dry their juice and make them equally brown.

Nutritional Information:
Calories: 636.6, Sodium: 1238.3 mg, Carbohydrates: 7.4 g, Protein: 36.8 g, Calcium: 348.2 mg, Iron: 2 mg, Fat: 52.8 g

Recipe 67: Tortilla and Cheesy Casserole

Total Time: 30 minutes
Servings: 4
Ingredients:
- Salsa: 1 cup
- Refried beans: 16 ounces
- Diced onion: ¾
- Cheddar cheese (shredded): 2 cups
- Flour tortillas (10 inches): 5

Directions:
1.   Preheat your oven to almost 375 °F. Spray one pie pan (9-inch) with a cooking spray.
2.   Cook onions and refried beans in a greased saucepan on medium heat for almost 5 minutes.
3.   Put one tortilla in the base of greased pan and spread bean mixture (1/3 mixture for one tortilla) and layer one tablespoon salsa over bean mixture.
4.   Equally spread one handful of cheese over salsa. Replicate this procedure and spread these layers on all tortillas. The top layer of each tortilla should have lots of cheese and salsa.
5.   Bake in your preheated oven for 15 – 20 minutes to melt cheese.

Nutritional Information:
Calories: 383.7, Sodium: 1286.4 mg, Carbohydrates: 34 g, Protein: 26.8 g, Calcium: 215.2 mg, Iron: 2.6 mg, Fat: 16.6 g

Recipe 68: Creamy Chicken Salsa

Total Time: 45 minutes
Servings: 4
Ingredients:
- Cheddar cheese (shredded): 1 cup
- Chicken (boneless and skinless): 4 breasts (halves)
- Sour cream: 2 tablespoons
- Taco seasoning blend: 4 teaspoons
- Salsa: 1 cup

Directions:
1. Preheat your oven to almost 375 °F. Lightly grease one baking dish (9x13-inch).
2. Put chicken breasts on greased pan and season chicken breasts with taco seasoning and pour salsa over chicken pieces.
3. Bake in your preheated oven for almost 25 – 35 minutes to tender chicken. Sprinkle baked chicken with cheese and bake again for approximately 3 – 5 minutes to melt cheese.
4. Top chicken with some sour cream and serve.

Nutritional Information:
Calories: 286.7, Sodium: 863.1 mg, Carbohydrates: 6.8 g, Protein: 35.5 g, Calcium: 242.5 mg, Iron: 1.3 mg, Fat: 12.4 g

Recipe 69: Broiled Fish with Brown Sugar

Total Time: 15 minutes

Servings: 4

Ingredients:

- Brown sugar (light and packed): ¼ cup
- 4 Salmon fillets (boneless): 6 ounces
- Black pepper (ground) and salt: as per your taste
- Dijon mustard: 2 tablespoons

Directions:

1.   Preheat broiler of your oven and set an oven rack at almost six inches from heat source. Grease the rack of broiler pan with nonstick cooking spray.

2.   Season salmon with pepper and salt, and arrange on your greased broiler pan. Whisk Dijon mustard and brown sugar together in one bowl and spoon this mixture equally over salmon fillets.

3.   Cook fish under your preheated broiler for almost 10 – 15 minutes, until tender and easy to flake.

Nutritional Information:

Calories: 329.9, Sodium: 310 mg, Carbohydrates: 15 g, Protein: 29 g, Calcium: 31.1 mg, Iron: 0.5 mg, Fat: 16.2 g

Recipe 70: Broccoli with Cheese and Egg Noodles

Total Time: 30 minutes
Servings: 8
Ingredients:
- Cottage cheese: 2 cups
- Egg noodles: 16 ounces
- Cheddar cheese (shredded): 2 cups
- Broccoli (cut florets): 1 head

Directions:
1.   Preheat your oven to almost 350 °F.
2.   Boil slightly salted water in one pot and add noodles to cook for nearly 8 – 10 minutes, up to al dente and drain.
3.   Steam broccoli to make it tender and green for almost 5 – 10 minutes. Combine cottage cheese, pasta, and broccoli in one baking dish (2-quart). Mix all ingredients well.
4.   Sprinkle cheddar cheese over pasta mixture and bake for almost 8 – 10 minutes to make cheese bubbly. Serve hot.

Nutritional Information:
Calories: 235.2, Sodium: 407.6 mg, Carbohydrates: 25.6 g, Protein: 13.2 g, Calcium: 301.9 mg, Iron: 2.3 mg, Fat: 10.3 g

Recipe 71: Easy Frittata

Total Time: 35 minutes
Servings: 6
Ingredients:
- Rosemary (minced): ½ teaspoon (optional)
- Garbanzo flour: 1 ½ cups
- Olive oil (divided): 5 tablespoons
- Lukewarm water: 2 cups
- Black pepper (ground): as per taste
- Kosher salt: 1 ½ teaspoons

Directions:
1.   Combine water and garbanzo flour in one bowl and whisk this batter to make it smooth. Cover this bowl with one plastic wrap and keep it aside at your room temperature for almost 2 hours.
2.   Skim maximum foam from the top of this batter and whisk olive oil (3 tablespoons), rosemary and salt in this batter. Preheat your oven to almost 500 °F.
3.   Put one 10-inch skillet (cast-iron) over a high flame until it turns smoking hot. Now pour olive oil (2 tablespoons) in your skillet and swirl to coat the base of skillet with oil. Continue heating until oil starts to shimmer and smoke wisp rises from olive oil.
4.   It is time to pour batter in the hot oil and carefully transfer this skillet to your preheated oven. Bake for almost 25 – 30 minutes until the cake turns brown.
Transfer to your plate and cut into small wedges to serve hot. You can sprinkle some black pepper (ground) on the top.

Nutritional Information:
Calories: 244.7, Sodium: 602.5 mg, Carbohydrates: 3 g, Protein: 15.3 g, Calcium: 215.4 mg, Iron: 1.3 mg, Fat: 19.1 g

Recipe 72: Zucchini Pasta

Total Time: 15 minutes
Servings: 1
Ingredients:
- Water: ¼ cup
- Peeled zucchinis: 2
- Black pepper (ground) and salt: as per taste
- Olive oil: 1 tablespoon

Directions:
1.   Cut lengthways zucchini slices with the help of one vegetable peeler and stop when you see seeds.
2.   Change the side of zucchini and continue peeling until you get long strips of all zucchini pieces. Discard seeds and slice thinner strips of zucchini resembling spaghetti.
3.   Take a skillet and heat olive oil over medium flame and cook zucchini in hot oil for almost 1 minute.
4.   Pour water and continue cooking zucchini for approximately 5 – 7 minutes, until it turned soft. Sprinkle some pepper and salt as per taste. Serve with your favorite sauce.

Nutritional Information:
Calories: 319.8, Sodium: 88.6 mg, Carbohydrates: 44.7 g, Protein: 10.5 g, Calcium: 84.7 mg, Iron: 2.2 mg, Fat: 11.9 g

Recipe 73: Bacon and Cabbage

Total Time: 45 minutes
Servings: 10
Ingredients:
- Bacon: 1 pound
- Sliced mushrooms: 8 ounces
- Black pepper (ground) and salt: as per taste
- Chopped cabbage: 1 head (large)
- Chopped onion: 1 large

Directions:

1. Cook bacon in one large skillet over medium flame and occasionally turn to make it equally brown. It will take almost 10 minutes.

2. Drain all bacon slices on some paper towels and let them cool. Once cooled, crumble bacon pieces. Drain bacon drippings, but secure three tablespoons from skillet.

3. Use reserved bacon drippings to cook mushrooms, onion, and cabbage. Cook well for almost 20 minutes to make them equally brown and tender.

4. Stir in bacon and mix this cabbage mixture well. Season with black pepper and salt as per taste. Mix well and serve hot.

Nutritional Information:
Calories: 203.6, Sodium: 332.6 mg, Carbohydrates: 14.8 g, Protein: 5 g, Calcium: 97.1 mg, Iron: 1.4 mg, Fat: 3.8 g

Recipe 74: Healthy Vegan Steaks

Total Time: 1 hour
Servings: 6
Ingredients:
- Cabbage: 1 head
- Salt: ½ teaspoon
- Black pepper (ground): ½ teaspoon
- Olive oil: 2 tablespoons
- Minced garlic: 2 tablespoons

Directions:
1.   Preheat your oven to almost 350 °F.
2.   Cut the base of cabbage and keep cabbage on the cutting board with its flat end downward. Cut into thick (1-inch) slices and arrange these slices in one layer on your casserole dish (select large dish).
3.   Drizzle oil over cabbage slices and top these slices with garlic. Sprinkle some pepper and salt as per taste and cover this dish with one aluminum foil.
4.   Bake in your preheated oven for almost 45 minutes. Serve warm.

Nutritional Information:
Calories: 93.6, Sodium: 229.8 mg, Carbohydrates: 12.4 g, Protein: 2.7 g, Calcium: 84.7 mg, Iron: 1 mg, Fat: 4.7 g

Recipe 75: Tomato Pasta

Total Time: 30 minutes
Servings: 8
Ingredients:
● Pasta (bow tie): 12 ounces
● Cubed brie cheese: ½ pound
● Chopped basil: 2 tablespoons
● Diced tomatoes (Italian style): 14.5 ounces
Directions:
1.   Boil slightly salted water in one pot and add pasta to cook it for almost 8 – 10 minutes, up to al dente and drain.
2.   Take one large saucepan and heat tomato on medium heat. Let it boil on low heat and stir in some cheese. Decrease flame to medium and mix well to liquefy cheese.
3.   Fold pasta in tomato sauce and sprinkle some basil to serve.
Nutritional Information:
Calories: 322.4, Sodium: 507.5 mg, Carbohydrates: 15.5 g, Protein: 8.6 g, Calcium: 51.7 mg, Iron: 1 mg, Fat: 25.3 g

Recipe 76: Wonton Wrappers

Total Time: 30 minutes
Servings: 72
Ingredients:
- All-purpose flour: 2 cups
- Egg: 1
- Salt: ½ teaspoon
- Water: 1/3cup

Directions:
1.   Whisk eggs in one medium bowl and stir in water. Keep this mixture aside.
2.   Take one large bowl and combine salt and flour in this bowl. Create a hole in the middle of flour mixture and slowly stir in the egg-water blend. If your mixture is dry, you can add more water (add one teaspoon water at a time) to make an elastic dough.
3.   Knead this dough on your floured surface (lightly floured) and cut this dough into two equal balls. Cover these balls with one wet cloth for almost 10 minutes.
4.   Cut every ball in 4 equal pieces and roll each piece into 10 ½ x 10 ½-inch square. Cut every square into nine 3.5x3.5-inch squares and use in your favorite recipe where the wonton wrappers are required.

Nutritional Information:
Calories: 13.6, Sodium: 17.2 mg, Carbohydrates: 2.7 g, Protein: 0.4 g, Calcium: 0.9 mg, Iron: 0.2 mg, Fat: 0.1 g

Recipe 77: Garlic Bread

Total Time: 25 minutes
Servings: 4
Ingredients:
- Garlic powder: 2 tablespoons
- French bread loaf: 8 ounces
- Dried parsley: 1 teaspoon
- Parmesan cheese (grated): 1/3 cup
- Softened butter: ½ cup

Directions:
1.   Preheat your oven to almost 375 °F.
2.   Cut bread loaf into thick (1-inch) slices without cutting them completely from the loaf. There is no need to detach slices from bread loaf. Mix parsley, garlic powder, butter and parmesan cheese in one bowl and spread this mixture between bread slices and on the top of the loaf.
3.   Wrap bread loaf in one aluminum foil, but leave the top uncovered. Bake in your preheated oven to melt butter and toast bread. It will take almost 15 – 20 minutes.

Nutritional Information:
Calories: 174.8, Sodium: 332.4 mg, Carbohydrates: 29.7 g, Protein: 5.2 g, Calcium: 25.2 mg, Iron: 1.8 mg, Fat: 3.7 g

Recipe 78: Chicken Wings with Lemon

Total Time: 20 minutes
Servings: 4
Ingredients:
- Lemon pepper (seasoning): 1 tablespoon
- Olive oil: 2 cups
- Chicken wings: 12
- Olive oil (extra-virgin): 2 tablespoons

Directions:
1. Heat oil in your saucepan to almost 375 °F.
2. Stir lemon pepper and olive oil (2 tablespoons) together in one bowl.
3. Fry chicken wings in hot to make the equally golden brown for almost 8 minutes. Check reading by inserting your instant-read thermometer in the meat and the reading should be 165 °F.
4. Toss chicken wings with lemon pepper mixture to equally coat all wings and serve with your favorite sauce.

Nutritional Information:
Calories: 287.8, Sodium: 239.5 mg, Carbohydrates: 33 g, Protein: 15.4 g, Calcium: 23.7 mg, Iron: 0.8 mg, Fat: 11.1 g

Recipe 79: Cheddar Cheese Sausages

Total Time: 40 minutes
Servings: 12
Ingredients:
- Pork sausages: 16 ounces (mild)
- Cheddar cheese (shredded and sharp): 8 ounces
- Baking mix (biscuit): 2 cups
- Bulk pork sausage: 16 ounces (hot)

Directions:
1.   Preheat your oven to almost 400 °F. Use aluminum foil to line one baking sheet.
2.   Mix hot sausage and mild sausage in one bowl until equally blended. Stir in cheese and mix them well. Add biscuit mix (mix half at a time) in sausage mixture and mix them well to make baking mix moist.
3.   Roll meat mixture into 1.5-inch balls and arrange these meatballs on your lined baking sheet.
4.   Bake in your preheated oven for almost 20 minutes to make them equally brown.

Nutritional Information:
Calories: 174, Sodium: 344.1 mg, Carbohydrates: 30.4 g, Protein: 6.6 g, Calcium: 97.4 mg, Iron: 0.5 mg, Fat: 14.4 g

Recipe 80: Spaghetti with Meatballs

Total Time: 45 minutes
Servings: 12
Ingredients:
- Parmesan cheese (grated): 1 ½ cups
- Spaghetti: 6 ounces
- Pasta sauce (tomato-based): 1 ½ cups
- Olive oil: 1 ½ tablespoons
- Meatballs (cooked): 12 (almost 1 ounce)
- Cooking Spray

Directions:
1.	Preheat your oven to approximately 375 °F. Grease muffin cups (12) with your cooking spray.
2.	Boil water (lightly salted) in one large pot and cook spaghetti in boiling water for almost 7 minutes. Stir occasionally, drain and transfer to a bowl with some olive oil. Put in your fridge for nearly 15 minutes.
3.	Take out spaghetti from fridge and mix parmesan cheese (1 cup) in cooled spaghetti. Equally divide spaghetti between greased muffin cups and arrange noodles in every cup to create small nests for meatballs.
4.	Top every nest with pasta sauce (1 tablespoon), meatball (1) and top meatball with pasta sauce (1 tablespoon) respectively. Sprinkle remaining cheese over each meatball and nest.
5.	Bake in your preheated oven for almost 20 – 25 minutes to melt cheese and heat meatballs and pasta. Let them cool for 3 – 5 minutes before transfer them to your serving platter.

Nutritional Information:
Calories: 490.9, Sodium: 876.3 mg, Carbohydrates: 65.9 g, Protein: 42.4 g, Calcium: 199.3 mg, Iron: 7.2 mg, Fat: 8.3 g

Recipe 81: Saucy Pizza and Pepperoni

Total Time: 30 minutes
Servings: 10
Ingredients:
● Pepperoni: 10 slices
● Mozzarella cheese (shredded): 10 tablespoons
● Buttermilk dough (biscuit dough): 10 ounces
● Pizza sauce: 10 tablespoons
● Cooking spray: as per need

Directions:
1. Preheat your oven to almost 425 °F. Grease muffin cups (10) with cooking spray.
2. Press biscuits (one by one) between your hands to make them flat and put each flat biscuit in one muffin cup. Press in the base and side of your greased muffin cups. Set them aside to set biscuits for almost five minutes. Slightly press all biscuits in the cups as per your needs.
3. Spoon pizza sauce (1 tablespoon) in every biscuit and top each biscuit with one pepperoni slice and mozzarella cheese (1 tablespoon).
4. Bake in your preheated oven for almost 10 minutes to make them light brown and melt cheese. Wait for ten minutes and take out from your pizza pans and put on cooling rack for almost 5 minutes.

Nutritional Information:
Calories: 125.5, Sodium: 438.9 mg, Carbohydrates: 13.8 g, Protein: 4.3 g, Calcium: 74.8 mg, Iron: 0.8 mg, Fat: 5.8 g

Delicious Gallbladder Sides and Sauces
Recipe 82: Green Smoothie

Total Time: 10 minutes
Servings: 1
Ingredients:
- Kale leaf: 1 (torn)
- Peeled orange: 1
- Peeled ripe bananas: 2
- Water: ½ cup

Directions:

1.   Blend orange in one blender and add kale and water in the orange mixture. Process again on high speed for 2 minutes.

2.   Add slices of bananas into the blender and blend again on a lower speed for 2 minutes to incorporate all ingredients and make a smooth blend. Pour into glass and add ice cubes to serve.

Nutritional Information:

Calories: 397.1, Sodium: 86.7 mg, Carbohydrates: 53.8 g, Protein: 9.6 g, Calcium: 285.1 mg, Iron: 3.2 mg, Fat: 19.6 g

Recipe 83: Avocado Yummy Smoothie

Total Time: 5 minutes
Servings: 1
Ingredients:
- Blueberries: 1 cup
- Water: ½ cup
- Peeled and pitted avocado: ¼ (diced)
- Almond milk: ½ cup
- Greek yogurt: 6 ounces

Directions:
1.   Add all ingredients in one blender and process well for almost 3 minutes to make a smooth mixture.
2.   Pour into glasses, add ice cubes and serve chilled.

Nutritional Information:
Calories: 305, Sodium: 229.8 mg, Carbohydrates: 50.3 g, Protein: 18.5 g, Calcium: 38.1 mg, Iron: 1.1 mg, Fat: 18 g

Recipe 84: Refreshing Watermelon Blend

Total Time: 50 minutes
Servings: 6
Ingredients:
●Watermelon: ½ (seedless)
●White sugar: ½ cup
●Water: ½ cup
●Cold water: 2 cups
Directions:
1.   Scoop flesh of watermelon and transfer it to blender. Add cold water and put one folder towel on the lid of your blender and blend for one minute. Strain this mixture through your fine strainer in one large bowl and discard fiber in the mesh strainer. Skim the extra foam from watermelon juice as per your needs and discard this foam.
2.   Put water (1/2 cup) and sugar in one saucepan over medium flame and stir well to dissolve sugar. Turn off the flame and let this syrup cool down at your room temperature. Stir this syrup in watermelon juice as per your taste.
3.   Pour this drink in one pitcher (2-quart) and put in your fridge for 30 minutes. Fill glasses with ice cubes and pour juice over ice. Serve chilled with straws.
Nutritional Information:
Calories: 72.4, Sodium: 1.6 mg, Carbohydrates: 16.9 g, Protein: 0.5 g, Calcium: 7.5 mg, Iron: 0.5 mg, Fat: 0.2 g

Recipe 85: Lemon and Strawberry Drink

Total Time: 15 minutes
Servings: 12
Ingredients:
●White sugar: 1 cup
●Strawberries (halved): 8 large
●Lemon juice (squeezed): 2 cups
●Water (divided): 7 cups
●White sugar: 2 tablespoons
Directions:
1.   Put strawberries in your blender and top with sugar (2 tablespoons). Pour water (1 cup) over strawberries and blend to make a smooth mixture.
2.   Pour water (6 cups), strawberry blend, lemon juice and sugar (1 cup) in one large picture. Stir well to make a smooth blend and serve chilled.
Nutritional Information:
Calories: 152.3, Sodium: 3.6 mg, Carbohydrates: 39.5 g, Protein: 1.1 g, Calcium: 16.8 mg, Iron: 0.5 mg, Fat: 0.3 g

Recipe 86: Mint Juice in Pitcher

Total Time: 20 minutes

Servings: 6

Ingredients:

- White sugar: ½ cup
- Rum: 1 cup
- Club soda: 1 liter
- Quartered limes: 3
- Fresh mint: 36 leaves

Directions:

1.   Combine sugar and mint leaves together in one pitcher to break leaves. Add lime in this mixture and muddle to juice limes.

2.   Mix rum in this mixture along with club soda and stir well to dissolve sugar. Serve chilled.

Nutritional Information:

Calories: 246.2, Sodium: 8.6 mg, Carbohydrates: 48 g, Protein: 0.6 g, Calcium: 18.2 mg, Iron: 0.2 mg, Fat: 0.1 g

Recipe 87: Honey and Watermelon Drink

Total Time: 5 minutes
Servings: 2
Ingredients:
●Watermelon (seeded and cubed): 2 cups
●Honey: 2 tablespoons
●Ice cubes: 5
Directions:
●Blend honey, ice cubes, and watermelon in your blender to make a smooth mixture. Serve chilled.
Nutritional Information:
Calories: 109.4, Sodium: 3.9 mg, Carbohydrates: 28.8 g, Protein: 1 g, Calcium: 13.5 mg, Iron: 0.5 mg, Fat: 0.2 g

Recipe 88: Chocolate and Peanut Butter Treats

Total Time: 1 hour 30 minutes
Servings: 16
Ingredients:
- Melted peanut butter: 1 cup
- Cold milk: 1 ½ cups
- Graham crackers (broken into halves): 16 whole
- Instant pudding mix (chocolate): 3.9 ounces

Directions:
1. Combine pudding mix and milk in one bowl and whisk constantly to dissolve pudding for almost two minutes. Whisk peanut butter (melted) in pudding mixture.
2. Chill this mixture in your fridge for almost three minutes.
3. Spread almost pudding mix (1 tablespoon) on every graham cracker and sandwich this square with another square. Make approximately 16 filled squares and arrange on your baking sheet. Cover with one plastic wrap and chill in your freezer for one hour.
4. Store them in your plastic bag and put this bag in the freezer.

Nutritional Information:
Calories: 482, Sodium: 284 mg, Carbohydrates: 43.4 g, Protein: 8.2 g, Calcium: 22 mg, Iron: 1 mg, Fat: 14 g

Recipe 89: Low-calorie Fudge

Total Time: 1 hour 15 minutes
Servings: 64
Ingredients:
● Chocolate chips (white): 3 cups
● Dried cherries (chopped): 1 cup
● Almond extract: ½ tablespoon
● Condensed milk (sweetened): 14 ounces
● Butter: 2 tablespoons
Directions:
1.   Grease your baking sheet (8x8-inch).
2.   Melt butter, condensed milk and chocolate chips in one saucepan over medium flame. Stir frequently and cook for almost 5 minutes.
3.   Turn off heat and mix in almond extract and cherries. Pour fudge into baking dish and spread into one smooth layer. Cover this pan and put in your fridge for almost 2 hours.
4.   Cut fudges into square (1-inch) pieces and make 64 fudges.
Nutritional Information:
Calories: 78.2, Sodium: 19.6 mg, Carbohydrates: 9.7 g, Protein: 1.2 g, Calcium: 42.5 mg, Iron: 0 mg, Fat: 3.9 g

Recipe 90: Pretzel Sweets with Chocolate

Total Time: 22 minutes
Servings: 40
Ingredients:
- Candy-coated chocolate pieces (milk chocolate): 1.69 ounces
- Pretzel twists: 15 ounces
- Chocolate milk candy (kisses): 8 ounces (unwrapped)

Directions:
1.   Preheat your oven to almost 175 °F.
2.   Arrange pretzel twists on your baking sheet and put one candy kiss in the middle of every pretzel.
3.   Warm them in your preheated oven for almost 2 minutes and put chocolate pieces (candy-coated) on the top of candy kiss (over each pretzel). Chill in the fridge for ten minutes.

Nutritional Information:
Calories: 36.5, Sodium: 11.8 mg, Carbohydrates: 4.5 g, Protein: 0.5 g, Calcium: 12.2 mg, Iron: 0.1 mg, Fat: 2 g

Recipe 91: Delicious Mousse Pie

Total Time: 3 hours 30 minutes
Servings: 10
Ingredients:
● Whipping cream (heavy): 2 cups
● Miniature marshmallows: 1 ½ cups
● Pie shell (baked): 9 inches
● Chocolate candy (milk): 7 ounces
● Milk: ½ cup

Directions:

1.   Heat milk, chocolate candy and marshmallows in one saucepan over a low flame to melt chocolate and marshmallows. Stir constantly and let this mixture cool down.

2.   Whisk heavy cream in one large bowl to make a stiff peak and gently mix cooled marshmallow mixture in the heavy cream.

3.   Pour this mixture into your baked pie shell and put in the fridge for 3 hours. Serve chilled.

Nutritional Information:
Calories: 373.5, Sodium: 225.5 mg, Carbohydrates: 7.0 g, Protein: 5.4 g, Calcium: 79 mg, Iron:1.4 mg, Fat: 37.6 g

Recipe 92: Peach Cake

Total Time: 45 minutes
Servings: 12
Ingredients:
- Sliced peaches dipped in syrup (undrained): 29 ounces
- Sliced Butter: ¾ cup
- Cake mix (yellow): 18.25 ounces
- Extra butter: to grease baking dish

Directions:
1.   Preheat your oven to almost 350 °F. Grease one baking dish with butter (9x13-inch).
2.   Pour heavy syrup and peaches in greased baking dish and spread cake mixture equally over syrup and peaches. Arrange all butter pats in equal rows on yellow cake mix.
3.   Now bake in your preheated oven for almost 35 – 40 minutes to make its top golden brown. Let it cool before serving.

Nutritional Information:
Calories: 227.8, Sodium: 173.2 mg, Carbohydrates: 28.2 g, Protein: 3.5 g, Calcium: 44.7 mg, Iron: 0.5 mg, Fat: 12.5 g

Recipe 93: Delicious Macaroon

Total Time: 2 hours 10 minutes
Servings: 8
Ingredients:
- Egg whites: 3
- Confectioners' sugar: 1 2/3 cups
- Ground almonds: 1 cup
- Sugar Substitute: ¼ cup

Directions:
1.   Line your baking sheet with a silicone mat (baking mat).
2.   Whisk egg whites in one bowl with a mixer to get a creamy texture and continue beating to make it fluffy and glossy. Sift ground almonds and confectioners' sugar in one separate bowl and fold this mixture into egg whites, almost 30 strokes required.
3.   Spoon a small quantity of batter in one plastic bag with cut-off corner and pipe one test batter disk (1 ½ inches diameter) on your lined baking sheet. If the disc can hold its beak instead of becoming flat, gently fold the batter for 5 minutes and test it again.
4.   Once the batter is ready to immediately flatten into one equal disk, spoon into one pastry bag fixed with one round tip. Pipe this mixture on the baking sheet in small rounds and leave some space between discs. Leave these cookies at your room temperature for 1 hour.
5.   Preheat your oven to almost 285 °F.
6.   Bake these cookies to set for nearly 10 minutes and let them cool down before filling.

Nutritional Information:
Calories: 71.4, Sodium: 34.5 mg, Carbohydrates: 18.6 g, Protein: 1 g, Calcium: 0.8 mg, Iron: 0 mg, Fat: 0 g

Recipe 94: Hummus with Olives

Servings: 8
Total Time: 5 minutes
Ingredients:
- Salt: ½ teaspoon
- Garlic: 1 clove
- Cayenne pepper: ¼ teaspoon
- Black beans (drain & reserve liquid): 15 ounces
- Lemon juice: 2 tablespoons
- Paprika: ¼ teaspoon
- Greek olives: 10
- Tahini: 1 ½ tablespoons
- Ground cumin: ¾ teaspoon

Directions:

1.   Mince garlic in your food processor and add reserved liquid (2 tablespoons), black beans, lemon juice (2 tablespoons), cumin (1/2 teaspoon), tahini, salt (1/2 teaspoon) and cayenne pepper (1/8 teaspoon) in this blender.

2.   Blend them well and scrape down sides. Add extra liquid and seasoning as per taste, garnish with olives and paprika, serve.

Nutritional Information:
Calories: 81.2, Sodium: 426.9 mg, Carbohydrates: 10.5 g, Protein: 3.15 g, Calcium: 26.5 mg, Iron: 1.3 mg, Fat: 3.1 g

Recipe 95: Healthy Dip

Servings: 20
Total Time: 40 minutes
Ingredients:
- Dried parsley: 2 tablespoons
- Softened cream cheese: 8 ounce
- Sour cream: 1 cup
- Green onions (chopped): ¼ cup
- Cheddar cheese (shredded): 8 ounces
- Refried beans: 16 ounces
- Monterey cheese (jack): 8 ounces (Shredded)
- Taco seasoning blend/mix: 1 ounce
- Hot sauce (pepper): 5 drops

Directions:
1. Preheat your oven to almost 350 °F.
2. Blend sour cream and cream cheese in one medium bowl. Stir in refried beans, hot sauce, green onions, parsley, taco seasoning, Monterey cheese (1/2) and cheddar cheese (1/2).
3. Mix them well and transfer this blend to one greased baking dish (8x12-inch).
4. Top with remaining cheeses and bake in your preheated oven for almost 20 – 30 minutes to make cheese light brown.

Nutritional Information:
Calories: 95.9, Sodium: 512.4 mg, Carbohydrates: 18.2 g, Protein: 5.3 g, Calcium: 27.9 mg, Iron: 0.6 mg, Fat: 3 g

Recipe 96: Jalapeno Cream Spread

Servings: 32
Total Time: 13 minutes
Ingredients:
- Jalapeno peppers (diced and drained): 2 ounces
- Softened cream cheese: 8 ounces
- Parmesan cheese (grated): 1 cup
- Mayonnaise: 1 cup
- Green chilies (drained and chopped): 4 ounces

Directions:
1.   Stir mayonnaise and cream cheese in one bowl to make a smooth mixture. Stir in jalapeno peppers and green chiles.
2.   Pour this mixture in one microwave-safe dish and sprinkle some parmesan cheese.
3.   Microwave on nearly high temperature for almost three minutes and serve.

Nutritional Information:
Calories: 110.2, Sodium: 189 mg, Carbohydrates: 1 g, Protein: 2.1 g, Calcium: 40.1 mg, Iron: 0.3 mg, Fat: 11.1 g

Recipe 97: Cheesy Dip

Servings: 9
Total Time: 1 hour 35 minutes
Ingredients:
●Softened cream cheese: 8 ounces
●Italian crusty bread: 1 pound round loaf
●Sour cream: 1 cup
●Salsa: 1 cup
●Cheddar cheese (shredded): 1 ½ cups
Directions:
1.   Preheat your oven to almost 350 °F.
2.   Cut one circle of bread from the top and scoop out its inner content to make it hollow. Tear the inside bread into small pieces to use for dipping. Reserve scooped out bread.
3.   Combine sour cream, cream cheese, cheddar cheese and salsa in one mixing bowl and spoon this mixture in the bread bowl. Put the top back on this bread bowl and wrap this bread in one aluminum foil.
4.   Bake for almost 1 ½ hours and serve warm with bread pieces (reserved).
Nutritional Information:
Calories: 362.1, Sodium: 691.2 mg, Carbohydrates: 25 g, Protein: 12.1 g,
Calcium: 235.5 mg, Iron: 2.5 mg, Fat: 21.3 g

Recipe 98: Hot Sauce

Servings: 30
Total Time: 30 minutes
Ingredients:
- Lime juice: Squeeze 2 limes
- Habanero peppers: 15
- Vegetable oil: 2 tablespoons
- Mango (peeled, remove seed and chopped): 1 small
- Mustard powder (dry): ¼ cup
- Chopped onion: 1
- Salt: 1 tablespoon
- Chopped green onions: 3
- Curry powder: 1 teaspoon
- Chopped garlic: 2 cloves
- Lime zest (grated): ½ teaspoon
- White vinegar (distilled): 1 ½ cups

Directions:
1.   Make sure to wear disposable gloves to protect your hands and don't touch any part of your skin and eyes with your hands while working with habanero peppers.
2.   Put garlic, green onions, onion, mango and habanero peppers in one blender. Pour in vegetable oil, lime juice, and vinegar.
3.   Cover this blender and pulse to make a fine mixture. Stop mixer and add in lime zest, curry powder, salt, and dry mustard powder.
4.   Blend again to make a smooth sauce and pour this sauce into clean jars. Store in your fridge for later use.

Nutritional Information:
Calories: 7.5, Sodium: 70.2 mg, Carbohydrates: 0.5 g, Protein: 0.3 g, Calcium: 2.3 mg, Iron: 0.1 mg, Fat: 0.3 g

Recipe 99: Pesto Sauce

Total Time: 12 minutes
Servings: 6
Ingredients:
● Almonds: ¼ cup
● Olive oil: ½ cup
● Ground nutmeg: 1 pinch
● Garlic: 3 cloves
● Pepper and salt: as per taste
● Basil leaves (fresh): 1 ½ cups
Directions:
1.   Preheat your oven to almost 450 °F. Spread almonds on one cookie sheet and bake them for approximately 10 minutes.
2.   Take one food processor and combine pepper, salt, nutmeg, olive oil, basil, garlic and toasted almonds in this food processor. Process them to make a coarse mixture.
Nutritional Information:
Calories: 91.2, Sodium: 56.1 mg, Carbohydrates: 2 g, Protein: 2.6 g, Calcium: 65.1 mg, Iron: 0.6 mg, Fat: 8 g

Recipe 100: Eggplant Meatballs

Total Time: 1 hour 10 minutes
Servings: 6
Ingredients:
- Olive oil: 2 teaspoon
- Dried basil: 1 teaspoon
- Dried parsley: 1 teaspoon
- Eggplant (lengthwise halved): 1 large
- Ground turkey: 1 pound
- Dried oregano: 1 teaspoon
- Sea salt: 1 teaspoon
- Shredded carrot: 1
- Black pepper (ground): ½ teaspoon
- Diced onion: ½ small
- Almond flour: ¾ cup
- Parmesan cheese (grated): 1/3 cup
- Marinara sauce: 2 cups
- Egg: 1 large
- Minced garlic: 2 cloves

Directions:
- Preheat your oven to almost 450 °F. Line one baking sheet with an aluminum foil and grease this foil with some olive oil.
- Arrange eggplant slices (cut-sides-down) on the greased baking sheet. Pierce the skin of eggplant many times with one fork. Roast eggplant pieces in your preheated oven for almost 30 – 40 minutes to make them soft. Take out from oven and set them aside to let them cool.
- Scoop whole flesh from baked eggplant halves on your cutting board and chop to make small pieces. Put these pieces in one large bowl.
- Stir ground turkey, eggplant chunks, black pepper, sea salt, oregano, parsley, basil, garlic, egg, parmesan cheese, onion, and carrot in one bowl. Mix them well to make a smooth mixture and slowly combine almond flour in this eggplant mixture. Scoop this mixture on your greased baking dish with your ice cream scoop.
- Reduce oven to almost 350 °F and bake these meatballs for nearly 15 minutes. Flip all meatballs and bake for ten minutes again.
- In the meantime, heat your marinara sauce in the pan over medium heat and add all baked meatballs to this sauce. Stir well to coat and simmer for almost five minutes. Serve hot.

Nutritional Information:
Calories: 354.2, Sodium: 769.4 mg, Carbohydrates: 25.4 g, Protein: 26 g, Calcium: 112 mg, Iron: 6 mg, Fat: 19.1 g

CPSIA information can be obtained
at www.ICGtesting.com
Printed in the USA
BVHW050857231121
622259BV00010B/787